'A vivid, evocative and resonant counterpoint of time, memory and meaning'   Joseph O'Connor,
author of *Shadowplay*

'Stunning. A work of great emotional and intellectual heft about how familial trauma and the collective past suffering of a nation can engender the nameless psychic pain of the individual. Truth and honesty shine out of every line'   Mary Costello,
author of *Academy Street*

'Magnificent. A brilliant combination of the personal and impersonal, of the collapsing of the two worlds one into the other. Spare, pristine, bracing'   Carlo Gébler,
author of *Confessions of a Catastrophist*

'Beautiful, compelling, thought-provoking. Mc Mahon draws us a kind of map for our broken hearts. An uncompromising reflection on what it means to be of Irish heritage today'   Tara Flynn, author,
actor and broadcaster

'*In Ordinary Time* is painfully familiar in its account of family loss and trauma in the urban working class.

Sensitively written and quietly devastating, it's the book I had been waiting for — the darker shadow twin of Marian Keyes' Rachel's Holiday'   **Niamh Campbell,**
author of *This Happy*

'Highly readable and quietly addictive, deeply moving and enlightening. *In Ordinary Time* throws light on a nation's traumas – the deep scars left by colonialism and the Catholic church – refracted through one person, one family'   **Priscilla Morris,**
author of *Black Butterflies*

'The best kind of memoir: a braid of the personal and political, the spiritual and global. An unflinching look at the generational devastation English colonialism has wrought on modern Ireland, it unfurls from one family's story of loss, love, addiction and redemption. Mc Mahon takes her place among canonical expat Irish writers with this extraordinary debut'   **Cameron Dezen Hammon,**
author of *This is My Body*

In Ordinary Time

Fragments of a Family History

Carmel Mc Mahon

First published in the United Kingdom by Duckworth,
an imprint of Duckworth Books Ltd, in 2023

Duckworth, an imprint of Duckworth Books Ltd
1 Golden Court, Richmond, TW9 1EU, United Kingdom
www.duckworthbooks.co.uk

For bulk and special sales please contact
info@duckworthbooks.com

Earlier versions of some pieces in this book previously appeared as
follows: "February: The Feast of St. Brigid" as "Brigid, Magdalene, My
Mother, and Me" in *Longreads* (November 2019); "April: My Mother's
Body" as "My Mother's Body" in *Roanoke Review*; "June: The Longest
Day" as "The Longest Day" in *Humanities Review* (St. John's UP: spring
2021); "September: A Day at a Time" as "Homo Spiritualis" was
shortlisted for the Hennessy Literary Award in 2012, and collected in
the *Hennessy Book of Irish Fiction, 2005–2015* (New Island, 2015).

A CIP catalogue record for this book
is available from the British Library.

1 3 5 7 9 10 8 4 6 2

Text design and typesetting by Danny Lyle.

Printed and bound in Great Britain by Clays.

Hardback ISBN: 9780715654477
eISBN: 9780715654484

for my family,
the living and the dead.

The center of me
          is always & eternally
                    a terrible pain—
a curious wild pain—a searching
beyond what the world contains, something
transfigured & infinite—I don't find it,
I don't think it is to be found.

It's like passionate love for a ghost.
At times it fills me with rage,
                    at times with wild despair.
It's the source of gentleness & cruelty & work.

                              —Alice Notley

Contents

Contents

List of Illustrations

Author's Note

The names of people and places in this work remain largely unchanged. In a couple of instances, it was necessary to alter an individual's name to protect their identity.

In the chapter 'December: The Longest Night', I am explicit about changing my brother's name. Given the circumstances, it was not possible to obtain permission to write about his life, or more specifically, the effects of his illness on our family's lives. After much consideration, I included my version of events here. In a book about Ireland's long history of secrets and silences, it did not feel right to omit this episode. In living through it, and in writing about it, I found no easy resolution. And so I remain, uneasy, in sharing it with you now.

Introduction

After I got sober, it took a while to start writing again. In 2011, I had a vague outline for a collection of short stories, little vignettes about the people I had met over the years while living in New York City. But then I heard about the death of a young woman who, like me, had emigrated to New York from Ireland in the mid-1990s. Her body had been found in a side portal of St. Brigid's Church in the East Village. She had gotten sober many times but was never able to stay that way. There was something about this news that kicked me in the gut. An image flashed across my mind's eye, a kind of map with a thousand points of connection: this young woman, St. Brigid, New York, the Great Famine, the Catholic Church, the English occupation of Ireland, the Celtic and pre-Celtic peoples of that land. It was too much to look at, so

I pushed it all away and returned to my manageable little stories.

At the time of her death, there was one picture of Grace Farrell online. It was taken when her son was an infant. He is seated beside her on a couch. The boy looks into the camera, and his mother looks at him. One hand rests on her belly and the other is raised up behind the child, as if she had been gently stoking his head. She is so young and slight, like a child herself. Her skin is pale and her shoulder-length hair is reddish and curled. I printed the image and hung it by my desk. I figured if this story wanted to be told through me, it would arise of its own accord, in its own time.

Arise it did. Shortly after Grace Farrell's death, the United Nations Committee Against Torture called for an independent investigation into the allegations of abuse against the Magdalene Laundries in Ireland. A hidden part of Irish history was being revealed, a terrible history of the treatment of women, especially those who gave birth outside of marriage. Grace was born outside of marriage, as was my older sister, so I began to think about our mothers and grandmothers and what they must have suffered under the church-state alliance that shaped Irish life for much of the twentieth century. There were glimpses, then, of why women like me and Grace Farrell might end up drunk and destroyed in foreign lands.

There is an old Irish phrase, *uaigneas an chladaigh* which means, "the sense of loneliness on the shore; a haunting presence of people who lived and died long ago." I found it in a small handmade book by Manchán Magan. He collected largely forgotten words from the coastal lands of north-west Ireland. I have experienced, as I am sure many people have, the haunting presence of people who lived and died long ago, but that there is a particular Irish phrase for this feeling gives insight into the culture and people. Just as words and phrases can get lost with time, so too can the connections that bind us to the people and cultures of the past. Without being able to articulate it, I had always felt the pain of this disconnection, so I set about facing the silences that caused it and began writing a reconnection to the ancestral past.

I dove deeper into Irish history, particularly *an Gorta Mór* (1845–52), the Great Hunger. In 2016,

I attended a talk at the Irish Arts Center in NYC. It was a panel discussion about the Famine. They talked about how an accurate account of Irish history had not been taught to young people in Ireland in the 1980s for fear of inciting further violence in the North. On some level I already knew this to be true because my own research had yielded so much more than what I had learned from the school curriculum, but the knowledge that these omissions were intentional, calculated, was new, and learning about this disconnecting force, in such a casual way, burned me up. Standing about in the reception area afterward, surrounded by my polite peers sipping their warm wine, I had to breathe intentionally and deeply in order to prevent myself from running amok and upending the place in a blind rage. After, we took the train to the Brooklyn Academy of Music to see a production of *The Hunger* by Alarm Will Sound. The house was almost full. Irish-Americans, I suppose, and Irish people like me packed in to watch an opera about the starving people of our native land. At one point in the tragic tale, I looked around and saw tears in everyone's eyes. What I felt, what they might have felt too, was that we have been cut off from this thing, but it is not yet over. We are not done with it. On some level it is still alive, still burning inside us.

I learned of Carl Jung's belief that being cut off from your ancestral past is a wounding. I knew so little of my own family history, never mind my country's history, never mind the women's history within it. I assumed, then, that no one thought it important enough to pass on; but, through the writing, I came to understand that my family's past may not have been discussed in our home because it was still so raw and painful. Late in her life, an old aunt in Scotland had mailed me her findings about our family on Ancestry.com, in the hope that I could help her find her long-lost uncle in New York, but it was in the drinking days, and I never got around to it.

Now, I pored over the births and deaths marked on my family tree, whose roots, like those of many Irish families, extend as far back as—and stop abruptly at—the Famine.

So, how to write the memories that still echo in the bones? I began with the mother, whom the poet

Nayyirah Waheed calls "my first country." My mother was in deep grief when I was born. As a result, my young self may have been troubled in ways I cannot access or articulate, but all the same I was disturbed by society's seemingly neat, convenient, "therapeutic" allocation of blame for our failings in adulthood to the mother. It is easier to scapegoat individuals than to examine or pull apart the structures that impact them. In my case, what rang truer was that my mother was carrying not only her personal trauma, but the trauma of being a woman in the suffocating Irish church-state of the latter half of the twentieth century. I wrote an aperture, through which I could examine the society in which she had been born and formed. The aperture continued to expand temporally and spatially, and it grew to include other Irish people, especially Irish women, throughout history, and all the way back into the ancient past.

I discovered the work of Dr. Rachel Yehuda, a professor of psychiatry and neuroscience. It was a revelation. Her research proved that both those who experience trauma directly and their offspring can exhibit symptoms of

PTSD. She found that overwhelming changes brought on by trauma rearrange physical systems, so our experiences imprint physiologically, and can be passed from mother to child, from generation to generation. Dr. Bessel van der Kolk's book *The Body Keeps the Score* was being widely discussed around this time. Kolk describes trauma as a singular event that overwhelms the central nervous system and interferes with reaction and memory. He introduced his readers to the Broca's area in the left limbic system of the brain. This area can shut down in traumatic situations. Since it is one of the speech centers responsible for putting feelings into words, the articulation of trauma, if it is possible at all, can be arduous and slow work. What is felt in the body may never be articulated in language, but its impact remains, moving inside us, waiting to be expressed under different conditions at another time. How then, I wanted to know, are our inherited, ancestral traumas to be released? Locating trauma may be a first step. Knowing how and why we hurt might help, but healing, it seems, is a journey through landscapes both familiar and strange that may take months, or years, or a lifetime, or many lifetimes to complete.

The title of this book, *In Ordinary Time*, comes from the Catholic Liturgical calendar. It refers to the time between the special markers of feast days and celebrations, and the extra-special time of Advent, when Eternity approaches earth, and Lent, when Eternity approaches consummation. The elevated language of the Mass fascinated me as a child, particularly the mystery of this phrase, because it refers directly to everyday life, where all the living gets done, where we are shaped, and where if we are women, we can be easily overlooked and forgotten, where our spirits can slip through the cracks of our religious and cultural traditions.

The concept of time was, not so long ago, different all over the world, but by the mid-1800s industrialized nations were unifying railway times, and by 1900, a standardized universal time had been established, fanning out around the globe from a central point in England, the Royal Observatory in Greenwich. People became obsessed with clock-time, and began to wear wristwatches and align their lives to this new system. This theme is explored by many writers of the era, but, to me, it is Virginia Woolf's insights into time, memory and mind that still feel most revelatory and current. What was covered less by those writers and thinkers was the fact that prior to that moment, people lived by sun time, and unindustrialized nations like Ireland might have had a subtly different relationship to the regiment of forward-marching linear time.

Henri Bergson stands out as another thinker whose name was once synonymous with the concept of time and who agitated against clock-time as an encompassing measure of human experience. While he was something of a celebrity philosopher in the early part of the twentieth century, his thought has since fallen out of favor, but I found in his concept of "*la durée*," or duration, a compliment to the tradition of the ancient Irish calendar. For him, one of the failings of clock-time was that it was immobile and complete, whereas time, he suggests, is mobile and incomplete. He wanted to account for the inner life of human beings, where there is a multilayered sense of duration which cannot be fully understood or defined by rationalist categories, but can be glimpsed with intuition and imagination.

The ancient people of Ireland had a cyclical relationship to time that was in conversation with the earth, the sky, and the seasons. For my ancestors, the day began at dusk, and the year at Samhain, going into the darkest months. The Feast of Samhain is a reminder that our ancestors and our dead are beside us. They have not been eliminated by time. These ancient people must have believed, as Bergson did, that time is not static, that it is an interpenetration of past and present. Their stories are still flowing through us from their very first telling, still swirling in and around us in ever-expanding and contracting spiraling cycles of time.

Part One
Imbolc

February
The Feast of St. Brigid

The city had not yet awoken on the frigid Sunday morning of February 20, 2011, when the body of a young Irish woman was found outside St. Brigid's Church in Manhattan's East Village. The news reports cited alcoholism, homelessness, and hypothermia as contributing factors in her death. They said that earlier that month, on St. Brigid's feast day, she had turned thirty-five years old. They said she wanted to be an artist. They said her name was Grace Farrell.

The following week, I ran into Dublin Kevin on East 10th Street. "Did you know her?" he asked. We'd arrived in New York when she did, in the mid-1990s, right before the Celtic Tiger turned the economic dial and drowned out what had been the background music of our lives: sectarian violence, mass unemployment, and rising emigration. But there remained other songs, muted maybe, sounds that take generations to rise up and reach the throat.

We ran away with a few hundred dollars and a few vague connections to join the lineage of emigrants from Ireland. People said, "Could the last one to leave please turn out the lights?" A joke to lighten the burden of history. In New York, I gravitated to the East Village to be with other immigrant kids who were writing poems and waiting tables. I knew, or half-knew, the ones from home, so how did I not know Grace? And how could this happen to one of us, in our own backyard, at a church built by our own ancestors?

In an Irish radio documentary, *Grace & Emmanuel*, Grace's cousin says she came to New York to find her mother, who had emigrated shortly after giving birth. The young parents were not married, and in the Catholic and conservative Ireland of the 1970s, that meant the child was often, as Grace was, given up for adoption. She spent her early years in foster care, and later, in St. Vincent's Children's Home in Drogheda, County Louth.

I do not know the particulars of Grace's mother's situation, but I think about her, and about my mother, and their mothers before them. The social climate of

Ireland in the latter half of the twentieth century was hostile to women. Divorce, abortion, and contraception were illegal. Married women were sometimes not permitted to work, and they had no rights to property in a marriage. There was no such thing as marital rape, and often the choice, in cases of abuse, was either to remain with the abuser or to become homeless.

Where does the story begin? Is it when the new Irish state ratified its constitution in 1937 to reflect its strengthening church-state partnership? When the institutions of social welfare were outsourced to the Catholic Church? I have difficulty reconciling their purported mission of care with the facts of their systemic violence. I have even more difficulty accepting the fact that the average person was in collusion: people like us, our parents and grandparents, our neighbors and friends. We believed the body of an unmarried, pregnant woman bore an unbearable burden of shame.

Women and girls could disappear, gone to visit an aunt in the country—code for being incarcerated at a mother and baby home or a Magdalene Laundry. At the mother and baby homes, newborns were removed at birth or shortly thereafter. Healthy babies were put up for adoption, placed in the foster system, or, in some famous cases, sold to wealthy Americans. In later years, if the mothers went searching for their children, or their children for them, they were sent down long, circuitous roads that led nowhere, or they were stalled indefinitely before a wall of silence.

In 2014, the *Irish Mail on Sunday* reported that a mass grave had been identified at Tuam, County Galway. It contained the remains of children ranging in age from thirty-five fetal weeks to three years. They died while charges of the Bon Secours Mother and Baby Home. Because they were seen as the products of sin, they were left to die of neglect and disease. Between 1925 and 1961 they were dumped in a septic tank beneath the grounds. All 796 of them.

The Magdalene Laundries were filled with troublesome girls. Girls who were too beautiful, girls who acted out, who talked back. Girls born in other institutions with no family to care for them. Dangerous girls who made accusations against brothers and uncles and fathers and teachers and doctors and priests. Even some very young girls who were never given a reason for their imprisonment. Some had their clothes taken, their heads shaved, and many were given new names. Outside, they were collectively known as "The Maggies." They did laundry from morning till night, interrupted only by meals and prayers. The word of a family member or a local priest was enough to get them committed. Sometimes for the rest of their lives.

In the 1980s, I used to take a bus into Dublin to go to secondary school. I often walked past the High Park reformatory and laundry, which was run by the Sisters of Our Lady of Charity. There was an iron gate through which you could see the austere buildings beyond. I never saw a single soul, but on some level, I must have known what was happening there.

In 1993, the nuns were selling a parcel of their land to a property developer. The grounds contained a mass grave holding the remains of 133 women who died while "penitents" of the laundry. While relocating the remains to Dublin's Glasnevin Cemetery, the undertakers unearthed twenty-two more collections of remains. One of the buried, a woman named Bridget O'Neill, was estimated to have been interred as recently as 1987. Some of the women had no records or death certificates; others were listed under their new religious names: "Magdalene of..." Many of the bones showed signs of physical abuse. One was even missing a skull. An iceberg had breached the surface of our consciousness.

I was a young woman in 1996 when the last Laundry closed in Ireland. The last mother and baby home shuttered its doors in 1998. This is not ancient history, and the time that has passed since only serves to move me closer to it, asking me to see it more clearly, to feel more fully the horror of it, in my bones. Women and children were not afforded the rights of citizenship, of subjecthood, of being. They lived under threat of being erased, hidden, buried. This is why my mother tells me—halting, hesitating—that in her day it was the worst thing in the world for a girl to find herself pregnant, but worse still was for her to talk about it.

My mother found herself pregnant in 1966. The skirt she picked up from the dry cleaner's was tight. She accused them of shrinking the fabric. She needed the pale-grey wool suit for a job interview. A neighbor who worked for Aer Lingus said he could get her in there. She imagined herself an air hostess—the most glamorous job in the world. She wore the suit with white gloves and a pillbox hat. Everyone on the bus said she looked just like Jackie Kennedy. She got the job. Finally, her life was coming together.

It had been four months since her American fiancé had been to visit. He could not believe my mother's family did not have a shower in their Harold's Cross council house. He could not believe they did not have hot running water. She had been organizing the wedding, but the Church insisted on completion of the marriage banns at Sunday Mass—over three consecutive weeks, a couple proclaimed their intention to marry as a way of ensuring there were no impediments to the union— and he could not stay for the required time. They had met on an American army base in Germany. He was a soldier and she worked the telephone switchboard. In the four months since his visit, the letters had slowed then stopped. She wrote and told him she was late, but she never heard from him again.

When my mother arrived at Dublin Airport for her first day of work, she was shown to the workers' cafeteria, where she was handed an apron and a hairnet. Broke and broken-hearted, she had no choice but to go to England. At least there, a woman could obtain an abortion, or she could give her child up for adoption

without having a lifelong stigma attached to her. She could, if she wished, work to support herself and her child. At least in England, she might have options.

I do not know what my mother had planned because she does not speak directly of these things. What I know of her story I have pieced together from fragments heeded piecemeal over the years. She went to London. She worked as switchboard operator. She rented a room. The kind landlady had known other Irish girls in her situation. I am careful in these moments not to seem too interested, lest she clam up and change the subject. I take what I can. I record the details, because I need to know her story so I can know my own. She just says, at some point, she began to love the child inside her, more than she loved herself, and this enabled her to survive. She gave birth to a baby girl and named her Michelle.

When life as a single mother in London became unsustainable, she called her brother. He helped her to come home. But it was my grandmother who ignored the talk on the street and ran to greet her daughter and granddaughter on their return.

My mother met my Scottish father in Dublin a few years later. They got married and moved to Ashbourne in County Meath to start a new life. My brother Billy arrived the following year, and Michelle, now a black-haired five-year-old, was delighted by the new baby. She went to school in the village, in a small school-house next to the church, and every day, my pregnant mother put Billy in the pram and walked to the village to collect her. My mother chatted with the other young mothers from the neighborhood as they stood about waiting for the kids to be let out. The school thought it best if the parents waited on the other side of the road, so a crossing guard was employed to escort the children safely across. On the very first day of this new arrangement, with seven children in the middle of the road, an oncoming driver lost control of his brakes. The parents and teachers looked on in horror as he ploughed into the children. Amid the screams and confusion, it was soon clear that one little girl was badly injured. A couple of local men were instructed to hold my mother back. She could hear Michelle calling for her as she was dragged, kicking and screaming, into Murtagh's Hardware shop, where she was held until an ambulance took the injured children away. Michelle died on the way to the hospital. I was born three months later. Six more children arrived after me in quick succession, a year or two apart, and Michelle's name was never spoken in our house.

I am beginning to understand why we might, at times, imagine our silence will save us.

Does the story begin when I had my first drink, around the age of ten? It was the recession-racked 1980s, and for a short period, my father, who had worked six days a week to support us, found himself without a job. That Christmas, Santa brought us all the same digital watch and an orange. We were not pleased or grateful. Poverty shrank us. We spent St. Stephen's Day at my uncle's house in Dublin. The living room, where the adults gathered, had leather sofas and Lladró ornaments. The air was thick with cigarette smoke that got thicker, and laughter that got louder, as the evening progressed. In the bedrooms, we scowled at our cousins, who called us *culchies* and wouldn't let us play with their Sindys and Scalextrics.

Looking back, I recall the feeling of inferiority and shame; was it our old shoes, the way we talked, or the way we grabbed at the crisps and biscuits? Or was it something in the air that seeped into our porous bodies? Shame is a word I can use to name that feeling now. With the name, there is context and clarity. Without it, the feeling rises hot and confused and choking. Billy was a year older than me, and we looked on while the younger ones laughed and repeated *culchie* words for the cousins: *waa-ter, caar*. We returned to the living room and began to clear away the used glasses from the coffee table as fresh drinks were poured. The adults said we were great little helpers. In the kitchen, we drank down the dregs of their beer, Bacardi and Coke, Jameson and ginger ale, and gin and tonic until our borders disintegrated.

This is what that first time felt like: a warm, golden circle of light expanded out from the center of my being and connected me to everyone in that house, and I was filled with love for them. I knew we were part of the same story that reached back to the beginning of time, and I knew too that everything was related to every other thing in the universe. Nothing was separate or alone. I felt all right, like everything was all right, and everything was going to be all right.

The world was changed thereafter. I had experienced something beyond the chipboard and linoleum of our home, the bare bulbs and the bickering, the sadness and anger that moved around the house like a vapor that settled sometimes on my mother's face, or ignited, suddenly, my father's temper.

By the age of thirty-five, I was on the treadwheel, running and running, trying and failing to get my life to move forward: eat healthily, work out regularly, quit the smoking, cut down on the drinking, find a real boyfriend and a job that pays a livable wage, but between the drunkenness and the hangovers, nothing could get done. And yet, there was the occasional radiance. That first-time-feeling had blasted itself onto my subconscious, where it remained fresh and unaltered by time or experience. Where it remains so, even still.

Does the story begin with St. Brigid's Church? It stands on the east side of Tompkins Square Park on Avenue B and 8th Street in the East Village. It is known as the Famine Church, because it was built for and by the huge influx of Irish famine refugees in the mid-nineteenth century. The potato blight affected all of Europe, but government mismanagement resulted in catastrophe for the then British colony of Ireland.

Many emigrants were young, single women. Arriving in the urban centers of America's east coast, they found themselves among the most vulnerable. The poorest people competed for physically demanding and dangerous factory jobs. Many young women found their way, or were forced, into the sex trade.

Irish women started to fill New York hospitals, sick with sexually transmitted infections and complications from pregnancy. The bodies of these women brought shame on the Irish Catholic community who were desperately trying to establish a foothold in the Anglo-Protestant dominant culture that despised them. The Catholic Church worked with charities to build medical clinics, temporary accommodation and job training for the women. They created an industry churning out domestic servants for positions that offered a shared room, food, and a small salary.

In the latter part of the nineteenth century and the beginning of the twentieth, Irish immigrant women thrived in these conditions. Some used their jobs as a stepping-stone to marriage or education. Others couldn't hack it at all, and regardless of their temperament, or their dreams, or their names, they were made into a trope, and they were all called Brigid.

You needed a Brigid. You got a Brigid. You had a Brigid. You compared your Brigid with your friends' Brigids. You laughed at their antics over luncheon. Such ignorant/willful/ungrateful girls.

St. Brigid was born outside of marriage in Faughart, County Louth in 451 CE. Faughart is a thirty-minute drive from where Grace Farrell grew up. Brigid was fostered out to a local druid and educated by him, but Christianity was spreading, and she converted. She became a nun and established a double monastery to house monks and nuns. She also established Ireland's first art school on the grounds. Her hospitality was legendary, and the monastery became a social and cultural center

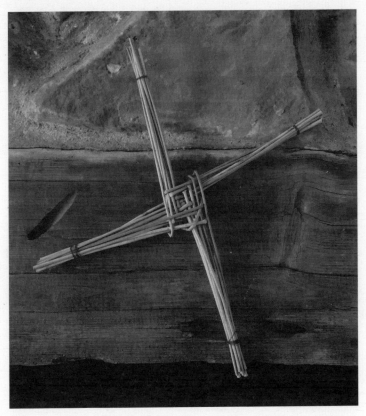

that hosted visitors from all over the world. In a poem attributed to her, she yearns for eternity and radiance; she dreams of getting drunk with God:

> I'd sit with the men, the women and God
> There by the lake of beer
> We'd be drinking good health forever
> And every drop would be a prayer.

At the time of her death on February 1, 525 CE (her feast day), she was the most powerful person in Ireland. She was eventually overshadowed by her male counterpart, Patrick, and the Catholic hierarchy reduced this complex and brilliant woman to a kindly maid. But, with her particular mix of paganism and non-Roman Christianity, she remained in the hearts of Irish women, and emigrants carried her far and away with them. Today, as the Catholic Church falters, devotion to this saint continues to flourish outside and beyond it. She is, among other things, patron saint of children born outside of marriage, of fugitives and poets, and maybe this is why Grace Farrell sought her out on the last night of her life.

Ireland has changed since I left in the 1990s. There is all kinds of diversity, there is marriage equality, and divorce and abortion are legal. The Catholic Church has lost its hold, but reparations and redress have been thin and late coming. Given the current reckoning with our history, I struggle to understand how the state is able to enact old policies on asylum seekers, a new and vulnerable population. In direct provision, the heavily criticized system that is supposed to provide temporary accommodation, people from broken and war-torn places speak of years bleeding into years, they speak of sexual, physical, mental, and emotional abuse. They tell stories of loss, of lives lived out of time; curfewed, controlled, stunted. Until recently, they have not been allowed to attend college, and they are only permitted to work after surmounting considerable hurdles. They speak of separated families and deep depressions. They speak of Sylva Tukula, a South African transgender woman in her thirties, who was being detained at an all-male direct provision center in County Galway. She died in 2018 following a brief illness. Her remains were detained for a period of investigation, after which she was buried in a pauper's plot. Her family and friends were not present. They had not been notified of the time or place.

On July 2, 2019, I attended a protest in the East Village. Stories had been emerging from the US detainment camps on the Mexican border: stories of overcrowding, of children caring for toddlers, of no soap or water, no toys or toothbrushes. The protest was scheduled for one p.m. Lunch hour. Slip out, do your civic duty. Slip back to work. This was how we lived. We did what we could. Someone passed around a roll of aluminum foil from which we tore little sheets to wave in solidarity with caged children huddled beneath aluminum blankets. There were the usual Fuck-Trumpers, as if this evil were the impulse of a single individual. What will we say to these children and their children, who are already writing poems about us?

In an *On Being* podcast interview with Krista Tippett, I heard Dr. Rachel Yehuda talk about how stress and trauma from cataclysmic and not so cataclysmic events can be passed on biologically from one generation to the next. One need not survive a war, genocide, or famine to have one's physical systems rearranged. But, she emphasizes, we are not in biological prison: experiences and events in our environment can also make positive changes to our programming. We can move consciously toward healing. And we can begin by talking. There is restorative power in the intimate exchange of speaking and listening, hearing and being heard.

Like many early Christian saints, St. Brigid's life was written about by the monks of the Middle Ages. They overlaid lives like hers with the myths of pre-Celtic deities, and used them as teaching tools to convert a deeply pagan people. The ancient mother-goddess Brigid was a member of the Tuatha dé Danann, people of the sun-goddess Danu, who were early inhabitants of the island of Ireland. It is not clear where they originated, maybe Austria, Denmark, or Greece, but legend has it they arrived in a great cloud. They were a warrior race of humans and gods who were skilled in magic, arts, crafts, and sciences. One of their sites is thought to be the five-thousand-year-old Newgrange, which lies a short distance from the towns where Grace Farrell and I grew up.

Brigid is the goddess of transformation, healing, and poetic inspiration. Her feast is Imbolc, February 1 and 2 (two days to encompass the full rotation of night and day). These dates coincide with St. Brigid's feast day—her death day—February 1, and Grace Farrell's birthday, February 2. Imbolc is celebrated at the midway point between the winter solstice and the spring equinox. This is the beginning of Irish spring, the time of softening. Seeds can take root in the dark and silent earth, where they will feed on the nutrients of their ancestors. The past, present, and future flow into each other like lines of the tri-spirals carved into the stone of Brigid's home.

When her child was killed in battle, the goddess Brigid invented keening: a low, wailing lament that rolled up out of her and across the land. When they heard it, the warriors laid down their arms. She invites you to join her if you have been blasted apart. From this mother, we learn the sound of our sorrow. We keen for our ancestors and for our children's children. And maybe this is where the story begins: when we lay down our weapons, open our mouths, and howl.

March
Imprints

They leave for America in the middle of the
night.
They could not pay their taxes.
Who will be next? the parents ask,
and say, *shockin'*, and shake their heads.

The Mc Dermots return from Texas.
Shelly is older than us now, because time moves
faster there.
She has cowboy boots and television words:
Vacation, she says. *Mom*.

We kiss in the big yellow digger
That is parked between our houses.
No work for the excess of rain,
and the trouble with the County Council.

We trudge through the fields and climb into
the ditch,
dipping our yellow buckets and hauling up
the slop,
we wrench tadpoles from their mothers, and
primroses from the earth.
And, laden down, we return home for supper.

Eight pairs of wellingtons muddy the mustard
linoleum of the little loo downstairs.
Mam at the sink, peeling potatoes, stares out
past darkening skies.
I hold up the yellow flowers, seeking, in exchange
for my labor,
the spark of something bright that almost kisses
her eyes.

April
My Mother's Body
(after Irigaray)

My mother and I rarely speak; I live in New York, and she lives in Ireland, but we are never really far from each other. Whenever one of us is sick or troubled, the other will call to say, I knew it, you were on my mind. If one has a cold, or a flu, or is going through a dark spell, we will say it is passing, passed—so as not to worry the other. Still, we can read between the lines, smell the air.

Grotto: from the Italian *grotta*, *grotto*, from the Latin *crypta*, "cavern, crypt."

On a visit home, my mother gives me a photograph. We are sitting on her bed going through the old albums. She is wearing a pale blue sweater and a pair of white jeans. Her hair has been freshly colored and her nails painted the pale peach of the moment. She

always keeps herself "presentable" at home, but she has taken a little extra care for my arrival. I, on the other hand, am going through a uniform phase: black T-shirt and black jeans. I don't want to have to think about dressing at the moment. My nails are cut to the quick, and if I remember, I will cover my grey hairs with a box from the pharmacy. Despite our opposing attitudes to appearance, we make the same shape on the world. People mistake us for each other in photographs, and sometimes, we even do ourselves. *Is that me or you?*

Sometimes, I see what my mother sees when she looks at me: a childless woman in her forties, never married, always busy; a strange bird who spends her days pecking about in archives, scratching out stories. She does not ask about my life or work because she does not believe in disturbing ghosts. Can she see what I see when I look at her? A mother of nine children, swept up into a life she never intended? I want to see myself in her, but I never wanted her life. We seem to be locked in a perpetual groove of reacting to our limited view of each other. We skirt and sidestep because we do not want to hurt each other's feelings, and so the distance grows between us: an umbilical cord, an ocean, a college education.

I examine the faces of our unsmiling ancestors for traces of us.

"Can I have this one?" I ask.

"You can have all of them," Mam says. "You are the only one with any interest in these old things."

"Who are they?" I point to the photograph.

Mam squints at the group of men huddled together in front of the house where she grew up on Mount Drummond Avenue. Their names sound like music to my long-term emigrant ears: Albie Murphy, Neddy

Bolger, Gerard Bolger, Bill Hennessy (my grandfather), Jack Mahony, Pa Neelan, and standing apart, my great-grandfather, Christy Bolger, the neighborhood money-man and a bookkeeper for the IRA.

The men are gathered to celebrate the opening of a Marian grotto. A small garden dedicated to the Blessed Virgin, where people could come to pray. A collection was taken from the people of the parish to commission a statue. The statue in the photograph was a substitute until the commissioned piece was complete. The photograph was taken in 1954. Pope Pius XII declared it a Marian Year to celebrate the 100th anniversary of the decision to make the conception of Mary an immaculate one. Almost two thousand years after the fact, the men in Rome agreed that Jesus could not have come from the body of an ordinary woman.

The centennial was celebrated all over the world, but it had particular resonance in Ireland, a country constitutionally connected to the Catholic Church, which had rushed in to fill the power vacuum left by the British. Ideas about the danger of women's bodies proliferated. They needed to be controlled in the Church/state union of marriage and put to good use producing more Catholics/citizens, whose bodies in turn would replenish a population halved by famine and colonization. All around the country, churches were dedicated to the Immaculate Conception, Marian grottos dotted the land, and baby girls were named Marian, Miriam, Maria, and Mary.

Where are the women? I ask. My mother shrugs and a familiar feeling blooms between us, a kind of chaotic silence that signals the end of the conversation. I want to know if their invisibility is a sign that they were excluded from all social affairs, or if they were just not bothered with the pomp of the day. Or were they simply busy making the tea and sandwiches behind those net curtains? But the past is off limits, even though it is here with us, in this room, all these years later, in a 4" x 4" image, the freeze-frame of an eternal present. Mam cannot go back to Mount Drummond Avenue, and I cannot make myself reach across the silence to ask her why.

Crypt: from the Latin *crypta*, from the Greek *krypté*, feminine of *kryptós*, "hidden, secret."

My brother Martin's Confirmation Day took place in 1986. He wore a red tie and a red rosette. In another

photo of the Mount Drummond Avenue grotto taken on that day, our younger brothers, John and Peter, stand at either side of him. The three boys are posed in front of the commissioned statue of the Virgin Mary.

They smile awkwardly for the camera because they are not used to being photographed. Film costs money, and shots are not to be wasted.

On Sunday afternoons we visited our grandparent's house. All the people who lived on Mount Drummond Avenue were old. The street smelled of boiled onions and marrowfat peas. Paisley pajamas and piss-stained long johns flapped along the clotheslines that criss-crossed the gardens at the back of the terraced houses. In the kitchen, my brothers and sisters sat on the floor in front of the telly and ate jelly and ice cream. Dad and Granddad sat in the old armchairs by the fire and discussed the football and the week's news. Sometimes Granddad talked about the time he worked in England. Coming home on the ferry, he would lose all his earnings on the horses or the dogs.

I sat at the table with Mam and Nanny. We drank tea and ate apple tart, like ladies. Mam and Nanny faced each other and whispered stories about women who suffered from their nerves. The smoke from Mam's cigarette curled back into my face, and I inhaled it and pretended I was smoking too. The gold mantel clock, the nail-art ship on the wall, the Spanish-dancer souvenir in her red and white dress on the windowsill, and the net curtains behind her, stiff with an old lineage of dust-mites busy about their day, eating, shitting, and mating in their polyester-blend universe, completely contained and unconcerned with our affairs.

Twice a year, Dad took us on a short drive to Mount Jerome Cemetery to visit the grave of our sister: in August for her birthday, and in December for her death day. Mam never came with us. Inside the graveyard gates, there were tall trees, dark with rookeries, that blew about in the loud wind. *Caw! Caw! Caw!* we called back to the crows as we ran along the curbs and breathed in the special graveyard smells: rot and moss and old flower water. We jumped and twirled with the little tornados of dead leaves. We kept an eye out for solitary magpies, *one for sorrow*, and if we saw one, we had to wait for it to fly: *one in flight is worth two in sight. Two for joy!*

Dad told us to keep our bloody voices down. To have some respect. We made our way through the maze of graves, careful not to step on any so as not to disturb the dead. We could see Michelle's grave from a distance. It stood out because it was so new and clean.

Our Beloved Daughter
Aged 5 Years

I counted three months on my fingers between Michelle's death day and my birthday. I figured out that I had been living inside Mam's body for six months when the car hit Michelle outside the old school. Nobody had to tell me. I already knew. It was a kind of memory from before I learned how to speak or to make a certain kind of sense of things. We blessed ourselves, said a prayer, and left.

Wait. I am here again. The memory accessed over and over. I add to it. I take away. The magpies and the crows. My father's exact wording. Impossible to remember the details with such certainty. The weather, how can one be sure? It doesn't matter. Not really. I don't think. I don't know.

We picked Mam up on the way home. She sat in the passenger seat beside Dad. The rain beat the bonnet and blurred the edges of the city's lights. The smoke from their cigarettes clogged our throats, so we could only watch as a silhouette of tears streamed down our mother's cheek. The horror of it: Michelle was real/is real. A chasm opened, and we knew our mother was lost to us.

I have asked my siblings: do they remember it like I do? Yes, they say, they remember. Then they say, "Oh God," and shake their heads. "Jesus Christ," they say, and shake their heads.

Trauma can be passed from generation to generation. We know that now. Vehicles of transportation include, according to the scholar of memory studies Marianne Hirsch, "narratives, actions and symptoms." The stories we tell and don't tell, the actions we take and don't take, the symptoms expressed by a mother holding the trauma tightly to herself, because she refused to burden her children with it. Still, despite her best efforts, it seeped out in slips of story and song. Whenever we heard the name Michelle, whenever the radio played that Beatles track, panic rose among us. We developed an unspoken code: we must distract Mam. We fought with each other, we fought with her, we fought to keep her face from falling. Sometimes, most times, anger is just grief that has forgotten its own name.

* * *

Carl Jung observed that children react less to what grown-ups say than to the "imponderables in the surrounding atmosphere." They unconsciously adapt themselves to the weather, which produces a correlative compensatory nature. My compensatory schemes involved touching and tapping things. One time, *tap*. Three times: *tap, tap, tap*. Walls, railings, tree trunks. And blessing myself: once for churches, hearses, and graveyards. Three times for holy statues, holy pictures, and grottos. I bowed my head. I avoided the lines in the pavement and the cracks in the road lest they opened up and swallowed me whole.

I found a dashboard St. Christopher at the end of our road, and I could not believe that anyone would discard such a sacred object. I found a Padre Pio keychain in the sweet shop at Woolworths. It contained a tiny relic of Padre's clothing. This was the beginning of my collection of Holy Things. I started taking them to bed with me, and before long, I could not sleep without them. In the morning, they were placed, for safe keeping, in the carved wooden box that my best friend brought me back from her holidays in Lanzarote.

Childhood was for other children. Death was my deepest and most primary concern. The death of the body was not nearly as terrifying as the life of the soul. We understood that heaven was hardly likely for ourselves. With any luck, we might make it to purgatory, and we could work our way up from there, otherwise we would be going to hell—for all eternity. Time without end. Our whole lives were geared toward avoiding this outcome: Sunday Mass, monthly confession, sacraments, and observations. We did the First Fridays, which ensured the presence of a priest before we drew our last breath. The school gave us a set of scapulars, which, if worn at the moment of death, would ensure entry into heaven. Best take all precautions. I blessed myself (three times) and genuflected in front of the picture of the Sacred Heart at the top of the stairs. Sometimes on visits home, I still take this reflex action, even though I am long-lapsed and the picture of Jesus, his wounded heart exposed, has been replaced by a mirror.

The Our Father
Three Hail Marys
The Glory Be
The Apostles' Creed
The Confiteor
St. Patrick's Breastplate

The Hail, Holy Queen

The Prayer to the Guardian Angel

The Prayer for the Souls of the Dead

Nightly prayers were said with focus and intention. If I drifted off, I had to start over. From the top. Occasionally, I pissed the bed. To comfort me through the confusion and embarrassment, Dad would say that little girls don't go to hell. Mam would say, there is no such thing. I didn't believe either of them, so I waded through the safety of days, dazed, dark-eyed, and exhausted.

My grandfather went to Mass every single day. He wore a three-piece suit and a trilby hat. He took up the collection and gathered the missals after the service. My grandmother did not go at all because she did not like priests or nuns. She shuffled about the kitchen in her slippers and pinny, saying, "Don't mind that ould fella, he says more than his prayers."

When my grandparents were born, Ireland was still colonially tied to England. Nanny grew up on Kevin Street in the Liberties when it was the biggest slum in Europe. My mind did not connect her to the history

lessons in school: the Lockout of 1913, the Easter
Rising of 1916, the Irish War of Independence, or the
Irish Civil War. I did not consider how she had survived
malnutrition, rickets, tuberculosis, or between my uncle
and my mother, five miscarriages. In the 1930s, Dublin
Corporation built housing around the city. It was the
new Irish government's initiative to clear the slums of
the city center. For years, my mother's extended family,
six adults and seven children, lived together in the
two-bedroom semi at the end of Mount Drummond
Avenue. They were grateful for all the extra space, but
they missed their old friends from the tenements and
the way of life they had known there. People looked
out for one another, Nanny said. Not like now, they'd
step over you in the street like they do in England.

On Sundays, when the national broadcasting
company RTÉ One aired the Angelus bell at six
o'clock, as it has done every evening since 1950, it was
our cue to go outside and give the adults some peace.
We joined the old neighbors in the grotto. Mr. Fox
and Mrs. White said we were very good children.
With them, we stood in front of the statue and said
the rosary. It was an agony of boredom, but we gazed
up at the twinkling star-lights animating the Blessed

Mother's face. The lights were a gift from my family, restitution, we heard whispered, for some secret and ill-gotten gains. Something to do with the horses or the dogs or the IRA.

Grotto is an angry word. I said it over and over inside my head, growling. I looked up and asked Mother Mary why she didn't help that girl who was in the news. Ann Lovett died in a grotto just like this one. She gave birth to a baby in the rain and the cold, and no one came to help her. The people said they didn't know. She was fifteen years old. I counted on my fingers: four years older than me.

"Did she go straight to hell when she died?" I asked. "For committing a sin?" My parents said no, but they took me into our front room and closed the door. If I ever got into trouble, they said, I must not be afraid to tell them.

Everyone stopped talking about Ann Lovett, but I could not separate her grotto from our grotto. Every week, I imagined her face blank, the rain falling, the blood and the dead baby in the cold grass. Every week I looked up, but the mother of the world was made of stone. Still, we petitioned her, muttering our prayers, rattling our beads: Hail, Holy Queen!

Secret: Middle English, from the Anglo-French *secré*, secret, from the Latin *secretus*, past participle of *secernere*, "to separate."

In 2018, when Netflix started streaming the Irish comedy-drama series *Can't Cope, Won't Cope* in the US, I settled in for a binge. If you don't blink during the first episode, you will see my grandparent's house with the statue standing out front.

Can't Cope, Won't Cope follows two friends, Danielle and Aisling, coming of age in Dublin. Aisling gets the morning-after pill for her younger sister, Rachel. Against Aisling's wishes, Rachel does not take the medication. One of the most powerful scenes comes in the final episode when Rachel roars, "I can do what I want. It's my fucking body!" When the series was made two years earlier, abortion was not yet legal in Ireland, and the morning-after pill had just become available without a prescription.

Clare, my younger sister, tells me about the time she was consumed by an inexplicable and urgent need to drive over to Mount Drummond Avenue. It was the late 1990s, and she had just found out she was pregnant. She was not married, but everyone wished her well, so she had no idea why, when she parked her car outside my grandparent's house, she broke down over the steering wheel and sobbed as she had never done before, or since. Was she moved by memories older than herself? Thirty-odd years earlier, our mother was there, with Michelle in her body. She was not married either, but no one would have wished her well.

When my grandparents died in the early 1990s, the family sold their house. On a visit home in 2019, I had a yen to see it again, so I took the bus over to Mount Drummond Avenue. Daydreaming all the way, like I used to, yielding to the muscle-memories of being in Ireland in April when the ground is soft and the rain is soft. Now, I like to feel my way down to the deep and tangled roots of things. Of humans, trees, words, stories. The ancestors and their calendars of stars; the spring equinox, the full moon, Easter.

There were Christians in Ireland long before St. Patrick arrived in the fifth century, but his is the story around which the narrative threads of Ireland's history have been woven. On the evening of the spring equinox, in the year 433 CE, the High King lit the great fire at Ireland's seat of political power, the Hill of Tara. This fire celebrated the sacred relationship between the darkness and the light. Agrarian people understood the spectrums and the interconnectedness of the days and seasons, of earth and sky. On the spring equinox, day and night are of equal length, after which, in the northern hemisphere, the days continue to grow, and with them, everything else, too.

The seventh-century monk Muirchú wrote in his *Life of Saint Patrick* that the law of the land stated that no other fire could be lit until the first flames of the sacred fire had been seen. But, on this particular night, before he lit the great fire, King Laoghaire saw another fire burning on the neighboring hill of Slane.

Patrick, the son of a Roman soldier, had been kidnapped from his home in Wales and sold as a slave in Ireland. After six grueling years, a dream showed him the way to escape. He vowed to return to the pagan land to spread the Good News. He lit the Paschal fire on the Hill of Slane and was preaching to the natives about the Risen Lord, when he was summoned to Tara to be brought before the High King.

For protection on the way, he chanted this incantation:

Christ with me
Christ before me
Christ behind me
Christ in me
Christ beneath me
Christ above me
Christ on my right
Christ on my left
Christ when I lie down
Christ when I sit down
Christ when I arise
Christ in the heart of everyone who thinks of me
Christ in the mouth of everyone who speaks of me
Christ in the eye that sees me
Christ in the ear that hears me

At Tara, the pagan and the Christian faced off. King Laoghaire's druids worked their magic and

Patrick performed his miracles. Finally, the druids sent a mist to envelop Patrick and his followers, but Patrick dispelled the mist, impressing King Laoghaire. He allowed Patrick to preach his new religion. Symbolically, Patrick brought the light that banished the darkness of pagan superstition and ignorance, but in effect, he took darkness off the spectrum and put it on a binary. The wrong side, the bad side, the side that needed to be denied and dismissed, ignored and punished, and so, the ancient relationship between the people and nature was changed thereafter. There proceeded the staggered and frayed end of an old order, and the uneven and unfinished beginnings of a new.

On Mount Drummond Avenue, the former council houses were painted and bright and the old cottages were renovated and rented out. Who can save for a home today with most of a paycheck going to the landlord? Everywhere in the city, there are signs that another kind of power has swept in to fill the vacuum left by the Catholic Church.

From a distance, I saw her outlined on her lone pedestal. There were no flowers to adorn her, even as we approached the Marian month of May. She was exposed; her stone was stained and her features weatherworn. Without the halo of star-lights, her head was as round as a baby's, and she was so much smaller than I remembered her to be.

When I returned to Ashbourne, my sister and niece were sitting at the kitchen table. Mam had put the kettle on.

"What did you do today?" she asked. A reasonable question, but I hesitated for a second. "I went to Mount Drummond Avenue," I said, and waited for the oxygen to evaporate. My sister shot a panicked glance at me, at Mam. I was perilously close to breaking our code.

Mam took four mugs from the kitchen cupboard and placed them on the table.

"What's it like?" my niece asked, and new air entered the room. A disturbance, a contingency. An opportunity for a mutation in our emotional DNA.

Mam took a jug of milk and an apple tart from the fridge.

"I saw Mr. Fox's house," I told her, "and Mrs. White's. They were these old people from the road who were very kind to us."

"Will you bring me there?" my niece asked her mother.

"We should all go together," my sister replied, cutting the tart open.

"The street looks lovely," I said, while watching Mam from the corner of my eye.

She turned around. "You couldn't afford to buy a house there now," she said, putting the teapot on the table.

"If you'd waited a couple of years to sell, we'd be rich," my niece said. An oft-repeated fallacy in our home. "Sure, how were we to know the boom was coming?" Mam asked, pouring our tea and taking a seat with us.

I told them that the statue was still there, and they knew what I meant when I said that the old house was the same, but all our ghosts were gone.

Part Two
Bealtaine

May
Ghost Girls

I could see the wound I had left
in the land by leaving it.
      —Eavan Boland, "Mother Ireland"

34th Street between Macy's and the Empire State
Building: when I arrived from Dublin in 1993,
Herald Square was filled with shoppers and tourists
as it is now, but instead of coffee kiosks and flower
planters, it was plastered with posters of a naked Kate
Moss advertising Calvin Klein. Kate was perfection,
but she was also a bit like us. A bit average. A bit
ordinary. I never said aloud, I want to be a model,
or I want to be like Kate, or more accurately, I want
to *be* Kate, because what I wanted didn't matter. My
obligation was to grow up, get a job, and take care
of myself, but there were ten of us in our house, and
by the age of ten, I was already exhausted.

In secondary school, there was William Wordsworth, and Louis MacNeice, and Patrick Kavanagh, and Gerard Manley Hopkins. In our textbook for the Intermediate Certificate, there were sixty-seven poets collected. Four were anonymous. One was a woman, but she was not on our curriculum. I wrote poems like the ones I read, about nature and nationhood, about lone shapes in landscapes, though I never envisioned myself as any kind of writer. Now we say, *If you can see it, you can be it*. We saw the young mothers of the neighborhood drag themselves, aged and dazed, through the supermarket. My friend's mother was confined to the house with a "nervous condition," and my own mother stood at the kitchen sink and stared out the window at some lost horizon, while we tore the house down around her.

I wanted to go to college, but it was an unfamiliar and faraway idea; I may as well have wanted to go to the moon. "Where would we get the money?" my mother asked. College was for people who could afford to sit around all day, *thinking*. I sat with them in The Coffee Inn under the posters and flyers: Nietzsche, Marx,

Simone de Beauvoir. We drank the same coffee, smoked the same cigarettes, but they knew these writers, and I envied them. Mam got herself a Saturday job at a women's clothes shop on Grafton Street. She could get me in there. For her, work was an income and an outlet. She got to put on lipstick and high heels and the dresses from the shop: mother-of-the-bride concoctions with peplums and puffy sleeves. She got to pretend she was someone else for the day, bouncing up Dame Street like she owned it. If I played my cards right, she said, I could work my way up in the company. I could become a manager, or even, the dream job, a buyer.

But there was not one item of clothing on the three floors of the shop that I would wear willingly. Every day, I changed out of my leggings and Dr. Martens and into my uniform, the blandest dress I could find, and every day, this felt like an act of betrayal against myself. All the women who worked in the shop talked about their boyfriends. They wanted to get married. One of the youngest was pregnant. No one mentioned it. She just had the baby, gave it up for adoption, and kept on working like nothing had happened. She could have gone to England for an abortion, but then, she could have ended up in jail if she did.

After work, the women fixed their make-up. Tilting their heads, they'd ask each other if the orange edges were blended. Then off to Davy Byrnes for G'n'Ts. Old men in suits paid for the drinks with greedy, grabby hands. The women pressed themselves in, hoping for a date, a house in the suburbs, an easy life, but it was never us they married, with our pretty made-up faces and our brassy blonde highlights.

The month of May, the month of Mary, the fire festival of Bealtaine, halfway between the spring equinox and the summer solstice. My friend's mother said, "If you wash your face in that morning's dew, you will find a handsome husband." It is the start of the Irish summer, and even if you pay no mind to bonfires and yellow flowers, you can feel the shift. I walked down the village in my long, black cotton dress from Miss Selfridge, dissociating and daydreaming my Kate Moss self into existence. A local photographer asked if she could take my picture. "You should be a model," she said. I joined a modeling school on Grafton Street, but they kept asking for money. So I spent my wages learning to walk, to pose, to have the right professional attitude. Charming and compliant. For a fee, I could go to the International Modeling Convention in New York City. I might win a contract. A way out. This was it! I took a loan from the credit union. I was all in.

I practiced my runway walk up and down our hallway. Pushing my younger siblings out of the way, "Move, for fuck's sake!" They just laughed and fired their My Little Ponies and Transformers at my back and head. I studied *The Face* and *i-D* magazines and posed in front of the mirror, taking note of my best angles.

In anticipation of winning a contract, I applied for one of the new American visas in the green card lottery. Most of the people in Ireland who applied for it got it, but the early scent of an economic turnaround was in the air at home, so some just used it as an extended holiday visa, and others let it expire in the envelope it arrived in. There were conversations about generations of Irish emigrants past and present, about our friends in Washington and the future of Irish–US relations. All of which was well and good, but didn't apply to me or the people around me. For us, the doors of opportunity opened narrow and brief. And on those rare occasions, we still had to push and pull and hustle and bend and scrape and sneak our way through.

At the convention, I did not see the city or the Hilton Hotel. My eye was on the prize. I was not leaving without that contract. I was burning with ambition, not to be a model, but to be a person in the world. To make my own life, whatever that was going to be. So, with young women from all over the world, I stood in a swimsuit in front of New York agents, while they glanced at the specs on our comp cards: Height, Hair color, Eye color, Bust, Waist, Hip, Shoe. I was not as tall or as pretty as the others, but I bombarded the agents with the force of my will. I scrutinized them for the tiniest crack through which I could squeeze the rest of myself. I got that contract.

Within a year, my green card arrived. I booked a one-way ticket to JFK. On the way to the airport, Dad said Irish families used to hold wakes for their children who left for America; with the distance and expense, they knew they might never see them again. We all agreed there would be no theatrics at the departure gate: A kiss and a hug, and a *bye for now*, a *give you a call when I get there.*

I wore a green suede coat with white fake-fur trim. Mam bought it for me as a parting gift. The woman in A-Wear said New York would not know what hit it when they saw me coming. "It'll keep you warm anyway," Mam said. "I believe it can get very cold."

The agency had an apartment attached to its offices on 34th Street, which I shared with another girl from Ireland called Tilly, a Twiggy lookalike with a blonde pixie haircut, and a very tall Black girl from Idaho who had been in beauty pageants. I brought five hundred dollars and everything I owned in two suitcases. I did not know who I was or what I was leaving. I did not know anyone or anything. I didn't even know Manhattan was an island.

The agency got us jobs testing for photographers, doing fittings for second-rate designers, working trade shows, and the student shoots and shows at FIT, but I was no model, and I never made enough money. We were always hungry, and when we complained to the bookers, they told us to do what everyone does when they arrive in this city: wait tables.

We wanted to move out of the agency apartment anyway. We spent a lot of time hanging out in the stairwell. The girl from Idaho ran up and down the steps for exercise, while Tilly hogged the cordless phone and cried with homesickness to her boyfriend in Ireland. I sat behind her, chain-smoking and reading a tattered paperback—*Tropic of Capricorn* maybe, or *Naked Lunch*. "Hey!" I called to Miss Idaho as she sped by, "how far is Greenwich Village from here?"

We pored over the Help Wanted ads in the *Village Voice*. New York restaurants required you to have waitressing experience, some even required New York experience. *Fucksake!* we said to each other. *You take the order, you give the food, they pay, they leave you a tip. How hard could it be?*

Tilly convinced her boyfriend to follow her over. He knew a guy in Woodlawn, an Irish neighborhood in the Bronx, who could fix him up with a place to stay and a job in construction. She was going to stay with him, and she invited me along. We planned to get waitressing jobs in some Irish place up there, and gain the experience we needed to find jobs in Manhattan. We could save for places of our own. We could start our new lives. We could focus, finally, on becoming ourselves.

It was a bright blue day when Tilly's boyfriend arrived. His friend from the North of Ireland picked him up from JFK, and they stopped by to collect us. We jumped in the back of a white work van and left Herald Square: the tourists, the shoppers, the workers, the sports fans, the Salvation Armies, the holy-rolly preachers, the pigeons, and all the naked Kates.

The sky stretched out as we left the city. Red-yellow maple leaves collaged the streets, and in the air, the smell of burning wood. We passed white-sided houses with young men out front, loading two-by-fours onto the backs of pick-up trucks. All lumberjack shirts and Timberland boots. The others bantered back and forth, and I leaned out the open window to mentally record every new thing: sights, sounds, smells; the triggering of a new story within me.

We pulled up to the driver's big, unwieldy Victorian house. He shared it with some other Irish guys. The house was crowded with heavy wooden furniture. Tilly and her boyfriend threw their things in their room while I waited in the dark hallway. Tilly returned and pulled me aside. The arrangement, she said, was that I would share the bed with the driver in his room.

Wait, what? But, I…

What were my choices then? I was running out of cash, and I needed waitressing experience. I felt myself slipping between the cracks of my old life and my new one. Suddenly I became aware of the fractional changes that can alter the course you are on. I resolved to do whatever it took, to figure things out, and in the meantime, to will myself through the situation, no matter how uncomfortable.

Sometimes at night, I woke from a dream that I was back at home, gasping for air. A return to Ireland was unfathomable, and life in New York City was so close, I could almost reach out my arms and embrace it. I missed my family though, and it would have suited me if they followed me over, but since that was never going to happen, I had to make my peace. I bought a phone card and called my mother from the phone booth.

"What do the women wear?" Mam asked. I heard her lighting a cigarette so she could settle in for a chat. I lit one too so we could be connected.

"They wear fur coats and runners."

"They do not!"

"I swear to God they do."

"I find that very strange." Mam said, and I pictured her perplexed expression as she tried to imagine such a thing.

"It's because they do be coming from their jobs on Wall Street, and then they have to get the subway, so they can't be running all over town in their high heels," I explained. "They carry them with them in a little shopping bag."

"I would have to wear my heels." Mam said.

"I know you would."

"Still, it just sounds like the most wonderful place." She inhaled deeply.

"It is, Mam." I exhaled.

The driver's room was neat and clean. He was quiet and serious—a sensible chap saving his money. I saw these guys in all the Irish places we stopped into. They sat alone and read the paper, the *Post* or the *Daily News*. Little flecks of cement stuck to their boots. Halfway through a pint, their features began to relax back into their natural, gentle expressions. You'd have to be careful, though, not to meet their eyes. The loneliness in them. Not the loneliness that is in want of company, but the one beneath it, mute and dangerous, a mirror of your own.

The driver did shift work most nights, and I fell asleep reading the Beats. Oh! The rapturous prose of *On the Road*. I could see their Columbia University in my dreams, I could see myself walking on campus in a tweed skirt and a woolen cardigan, moss-green maybe… mustard. Where was their Lower East Side of the cold-water flats and the poetry and love? Sometimes I woke up as the driver slipped into the bed, but he always kept a respectful distance, and I always slid out early in the morning before he stirred.

Tilly and I sashayed into the local pubs in Woodlawn. We looked down our noses at the Irish-Americans and the Irish immigrants who lived there. They were so committed to their "Irishness." Tricolors and trad music. They stuck together. Drawing attention to yourself was not encouraged in a mostly undocumented community. Them with the heads down. One eye always looking over the shoulder. Us with the fashions and the new Morrison visas—visas that were meant for them, but paranoia and fear of deportation prevented many from applying.

On the street, the people smirked and snickered when we passed. "Look at this pair," they'd say. "Who do they think they are? State of them, like." Nevertheless, word was sent out, as it had been sent out, through the community, down the ages: two girls had just come over from home; they needed work, and a place to stay.

"What are you lookin' for?" people asked us.

"We want to work in a bar or a club," we replied. We heard the bartenders in the Limelight and the Roxy were making five hundred dollars in one night.

"I know a girl in Yonkers who needs someone lookin' after her kids," one man offered. "We don't think so," we snorted in reply. We didn't come all this way to mind snot-nosed kids in Yonkers.

"Uppity fuckin' Dubs, the pair of ye," he said. Picked up his pint and hoofed off. We laughed and laughed, and then we were broke.

The driver knew a woman who worked at the Irish-American diner. She expected to be busy on Thanksgiving Day and could use some extra help. "What is Thanksgiving?" I asked him. He said it was a holiday the English had made up about sharing a harvest feast with the native people.

"You don't think it happened?" I asked.

"Not in the happy way they make out," he said.

I showed up to the Irish-American diner in my skin-tight red velvet jeans, my black mid-riff baring tank-top and my Adidas. A harried Irish mother of two boys—the consort of a lumberjack-shirted man who worked construction—was to train me before the dinner rush. "I have plenty of experience," I lied. "I worked in Dublin at Bewley's on Grafton Street and The Coffee Inn on South Anne Street."

"OK," she said, making it clear with a glance that the likes of me did not impress her. She was all business:

"Give them a basket of bread when you give them the menu. Take their drink order right then and there. Tell them the special. Today it's roasted turkey with stuffing, cranberry sauce, mashed sweet potatoes and green bean casserole. Are you with me? They get soup or salad to start. Find out what dressing they want. When they get their appetizer, tell the kitchen to fire the entrée. When you see the busboy clearing their dinner plates, bring them the dessert menu. Total the check like this."

Here she scribbled some hieroglyphics on a guest-check pad.

"Have them pay at the register there. Any questions?"

"Yeah," I said, "what are *sweet* potatoes?"

The look on her thin-lipped, makeup-less face. Her grown-out perm pulled into a stringy ponytail at the back of her head. Her functional jeans. Her oversized T-shirt with a nature graphic and the words: *No Man Is an Island*. Her pale eyes filled with cold intensity as it dawned on her that she was being made to deal, yet again, with a complete *Fuckin' Eejit*, and she would be forced, on this day, as I am sure she was on many days, to bear the brunt of the labor.

All of Woodlawn descended on the diner at the same moment. I could not get my bearings. I could not answer questions about the menu, nor could I remember the special. I forgot to take the drink orders, and I fired the entrées before the appetizers were served. I forgot to add drink orders to checks, and I gave the wrong checks to the wrong tables.

The shift flattened me, but I ate an enormous Thanksgiving dinner after and felt better. The first wondrous taste of sweet potatoes and pecan pie. I sat at the counter with the Mexican chef. He told me not to worry, that everything would work out. The harried mother divvied up the tips in a manner she thought fair, and I returned to the Victorian house with seventeen dollars, a full belly, and a firm resolve to get the fuck out of Woodlawn as soon as possible.

That night, the driver had been to the pub. He climbed into the bed as usual, but instead of turning his back, he looped his arm around me, naturally, as if he had done it a thousand times before, and I let him. I barely breathed for fear of encouraging further action, or discouraging this one. The warmth and comfort of another body. But I knew a turn toward him would have been a turn toward a life I did not want: the driver's girlfriend, the driver's pregnant girlfriend, the driver's wife. While I could not articulate the life I wanted, I knew this was not it.

The next day I called the agency and asked if I could move back into their apartment. Now that I had some waitressing experience (four hours) under my belt, I felt fairly certain I would be able to find employment in the city. I said goodbye to Tilly, the driver and Woodlawn. I would make my own way from there. I didn't need them, I didn't need anyone or anything.

Today, on 34th Street, I sometimes see that ghost of a girl. My god, how I'd like to tell my younger self, *I*

could not see the wound I had left in the land by leaving it, nor could I see the corresponding wound in me. I'd say, *I didn't even know Manhattan was an island!* I'd put my arms around her and tell her, *I didn't know, for a very long time, that I was not.*

June
The Longest Day

My little brother died in Ireland during the summer solstice of 1998. At the time, I was living far from home, in Brooklyn, NY. He was a baby who convulsed with laughter in his crib. A boy who could not bear going to school, so he sat with his back to the class and refused to speak. A teen who learned to play guitar so he could strum along to the Britpop anthems he loved. A lad who got a factory job and saved his wages to buy a motorbike. A young man who was fussy about his hair, his shirt, his shoes: Ben Sherman, Lacoste, Adidas. A little brother who experimented with drugs: hash, ecstasy, heroin.

In the decade after her brother died, the Canadian poet Anne Carson kept a notebook. In it, she recorded memories and impressions of her brother, along with scraps of letters and stamps she had saved from his travels abroad. She did this, she tells us, because a brother does not end. He goes on. Out of this notebook, Carson created her book, *Nox*. Since high school, she had loved the elegy that the Roman poet Catullus wrote for his brother, who also died on foreign soil. She juxtaposes the fragments from her notebook with a word-by-word translation of the ancient elegy. Carson examines the connection between history and elegy; they are akin, she claims. Herodotus was supposedly the first historian, though, as she says, he thought history was by far the strangest thing that humans do: prowling the past, making up stories, assigning meaning even to that which is incomprehensible.

After a short stint waitressing in an Irish bar on West 33rd Street, I had saved enough to share a rent-stabilized apartment on East 21st with another Irish girl. I also found a new job at the Temple Bar, a downtown lounge famous for its inflated prices and oversized martinis. The waitresses wore black leather pants and tuxedo jackets. MAC's Vamp lipstick made them look serious and mean. Most of the customers were Wall Street traders or vaguely recognizable celebrities. The staff were convinced that the customers gave bigger tips when they received a little attitude. A request for a glass of water might be met with an eye roll. Extra olives, a resentful glare. Anyway, the staff argued, how could you respect a capitalist fuck who would spend $10 (adjust for inflation) on a cocktail, get drunk enough to try to grope you, then throw up the contents of their stomach on the sidewalk outside?

The staff stayed late after the bar closed. They drank and argued and hooked up, and into the small hours, they did bang-on impressions of the manager, the owner, the customers, and each other. I did not drink myself, but stayed on to laugh along. I felt their brightness and humor shine through me, and I was delighted to be there among them. Brian, a lanky boy from New Jersey who was always drawing and making notes in his sketchbook, became a friend. During shared cigarette breaks in the basement, we sat on overturned milkcrates and talked about what we were going to do with our lives. He was going to rent a loft in Red Hook, Brooklyn and live there with his boyfriend, his brother, and some other friends. There was a big studio space in the back, and he was going to start an art collective. I could live there and join if I wanted to. I wanted to. I wanted very much to tether myself to something or someone, to land, finally, safe and sound, in this new country.

The reason I did not drink involved a secret deal with God. From childhood, I hung around with a group of friends, a gang of ten girls from the road. At age twelve, we had been coerced into taking the Confirmation pledge, which meant we made a promise to God that we would not drink until we were eighteen. I was the last holdout and remained dry until I was fourteen, then I joined the others in stealing mixes of the sugary liqueurs from the backs of our parents' drinks cabinets. We would meet up behind the old school in the village, or in our gang's spot in "the field," someone would bring the cigarettes, Carroll's or John Player Blue, and we would pass the bottle around. If someone had been asked to pick out the potential drinker among us, it would not have been me. It would not have been me in the mid-teen years drinking cans before the Saturday night disco, it would not have been me in the late teens sipping a glass of lager in Bruxelles or the William Tell, and yet looking back, all the signs were there. I read my friends' ability to laugh loudly and throw up in the grass as indicative of how carefree I thought they were, how comfortable in their skin. My reticence with alcohol stemmed from the strong sense that if I were to let go, even a little, it would take me, and it would take me to a place from which I might not easily return.

At that time, my two little brothers were inseparable. They had melded into one unit, and people took to calling them John-Peter instead of John and Peter. One day, the older of the two, John, aged fourteen, drank a bottle of vodka and jumped off the roof of an abandoned building. My father called from the hospital. He didn't know if John would make it. He asked us to pray. I was eighteen then, and I reverse-engineered the confirmation pledge, making a new vow and asking something in return: never to drink again, if my brother's life would be spared. In the morning, John had made a miraculous recovery and, inwardly, secretly, I thought I had something to do with it.

The Temple Bar offered an employee discount, so we often hung around the place on our nights off. One night much like any other, my French friend Valerie and I took a table in the lounge. She ordered a glass of red wine, and without forethought, a subconscious desire made its way to my mouth, and I found myself ordering one too. The first sip slid down my throat and on down into my soul. I felt myself illuminated from within and connected with everyone around me—I saw that we were all part of the same living, breathing organism, and that I need not worry, I just need *be*. It was fitting, perhaps, that such a spiritual experience should occur in a place called Temple. I was internally altered, and the external world became, for a time, a softer, less hostile place.

David was a Temple Bar customer. He worked around the corner at the Keith Haring Foundation. Sometimes he and a friend came by for a drink after work. They were boyish and shy in T-shirts and baseball caps. His friend told me David was sad these days because he was twenty-nine and going through a divorce. Whenever I delivered their drinks, I found I liked being next to him. It was nothing he did or said really, just an energy between us. I invited David to my twenty-fourth birthday party: frozen margaritas at El Sombrero and a show at Arlene's Grocery, a live-music venue, after. I kept watching the door of the Mexican restaurant, and only when David arrived did I realize it was him I had been looking for.

Later that week we had dinner in the window seat of Marion's on the Bowery. The place opened in the 1950s, and had maintained a kind of glamour that was having a resurgence. Girls with heavily lined eyes smoked Gauloises at the bar, their laughter mixing like melodies over Miles Davis tunes. I had caught a cold and spent the evening sniffling into a crumpled tissue. David invited me to spend the night at his Brooklyn Heights apartment. There was a second bedroom, he said. There was NyQuil and tea and juice and things that would help. In the morning there was a note: *Hope you feel better. Door locks behind. Stay as long as you need. Forever if you like.*

His apartment, unlike Brian's loft in Red Hook, was neat and clean. It was all muted tones and contemporary works of art. Big windows faced the East River and the magical skyline of the city beyond. There was food in the fridge and closets full of clean sheets and towels and extras of things you run out of, like toothpaste and toilet paper. There was a little black pug named Lucy, who was not altogether put out by my presence, so I stayed.

Nurturing came naturally to David, and I soaked it up like a parched plant. He made me a pot of Irish tea and brought me a fresh bagel for breakfast before he left for work in the morning. We walked his dog along the promenade in the evening. We made dinner and talked and laughed. After brunch on Sundays, we spent the day in the living room spread out over the *New York Times*. We went to the movies, met friends for drinks, and got tickets to all the interesting shows happening around town. Our lives expanded. I met his family and he came to Ireland to meet mine. When we fought, David insisted we not go to bed angry. I only knew how to be hysterical or to shut down, but he knew how to talk things out. We both felt lucky. With all the billions of people alive in the world, we had found each other. It was chance, yes, but somehow, the universe willed us to be. Finally, I let myself relax into the luxury of love.

Once a month, I called home to let my family know I was still alive. This was our ritual: I called, my mother talked about the weather, the other kids, the neighbors; I listened and said, *Uhm-hm.* So when she called the

Temple Bar just after midnight on June 21, 1998, I knew it was not to deliver good news.

"There's been an accident," she said.

"Who?" I asked.

"Peter."

"What?"

"You have to come home."

"Why?"

"I can't tell you over the phone."

"What can you not tell me?"

"He's dead."

He's dead. The words are the weight of a planet. A planet that rolls around the sun on the loosely woven warp and weft of space and time. The fabric gives a little under the tremendous mass, but momentum is maintained. If time were to stop, if it stood still, even for a moment, the planet would sink and sink. If you reached down into the fabric and plucked it back out, you might find the warp and weft intact, but much too stretched out ever to reconstitute its original shape.

Grief changes time. You no longer roll along. You wobble and stumble, you stall and stagger. You stand still and watch as everything else rushes past.

In David's apartment, I swallowed shot after shot of tequila, but the alcohol was not doing its job. I wanted to be obliterated and to wake up the next day to find it was all a dream. I insisted David go on to bed because I needed to be alone. The milky-grey light of dawn soured in as I sat staring out at the East River. I sensed my brother's spirit, his confusion and isolation, as if our worlds had momentarily dissolved into one another. I wanted to be at home in Ireland with my family, with Mam and Dad and my brothers and sisters. I was in a foreign land when I should have been in my own country, in the living room of my parent's house, drinking tea and staring into space with people who knew Peter and who knew me.

The flight to Ireland was endless. I could not watch the film. I could not read. I could not eat. I could not cry. I could not sleep. My skin itched and my heart ached. I'd forget about Peter for a minute, then I'd remember him all over again.

We went as a family to view the body. The nine of us filed into the cold mortuary where a corpse lay on a stainless-steel table. It was covered to the shoulders with a white sheet. "Oh my god!" I called out, instantly relieved. "It's not Peter!" *This is unbelievable*, I thought. *There has been a mistake, some terrible misunderstanding.* "Peter is just missing," I told my family. "We have to find him." They didn't seem to get that Peter was still out there, still alive. "This just looks like Peter," I tried to explain, "but it's not him, because Peter's neck did not stick out on the side like that!" I pointed to the protrusion as evidence. I searched their eyes. They didn't seem to understand. My father looked down. My mother looked away. This magical thinking in the face of death, this inability to integrate information with the evidence of your eyes, is a defense mechanism, triggered in order to buy time, the extra seconds and minutes needed, to process the incomprehensible, so that you can go on.

Somehow, it was decided that each of us should kiss Peter's forehead. I suppose we had to do something. This was just one of many strange rituals we enacted to help us cope with the unacceptable truth. The fact-ness of it. Peter's forehead, when it met my lips, was cold and hard and less animate than marble. *I read that somewhere*, I thought, as I straightened back up. *Cold and hard and less animate than marble. I read that; I know that. I have been here before.*

The doctor told my father that Peter and his passenger, his friend Hugh, did not die on impact. There was breath enough in them to receive their Last Rites. This was welcome news because it ensured they were in heaven, and someday, we could all be together again. Death was not final. Even if we didn't really believe it, we believed it because we had to, because we were taking any promise of ease from the pain, even if we had to wait until the next life to feel it.

Much was made of Peter's personal effects. The empty wallet, the lighter, the keys, the chain he wore around his neck. *Was there a watch? Where was his watch?* As if these quotidian things had taken on a new aura because they were "his things." Because they were with him when he passed over, and we were not. But, if we touched them now, and held them in our hands and looked at them long enough, and if we designated them to a special box, we could trick our minds into thinking that through these relics, a part of Peter was still here. The preservation and veneration of these objects would show that this human being, among the billions alive on Earth, meant something, means something, to us.

In many Irish towns and villages, even today, there is a church at the center. Across the street, there is inevitably a pub, a public house. It is interesting that the Irish translation, *teach an pobal* (house of the people) was an early Irish name for a church. Both church and pub offer community and common purpose. Both also offer a spiritual solution to the problems of being human and being alive.

After the funeral, we left the churchyard and walked across the street to the Hunter's Moon, where the local drug dealer bought me a drink and offered his condolences, both of which I accepted. He told me Peter was an addict. In a few short years, the heroin epidemic that took hold of Dublin's north side through the 1980s had spread to every small town in Ireland. As he spoke, I looked into the hard, dead set of his eyes. He was only twenty-odd himself. A boy from a troubled home. I remembered him as a little kid kicking a ball against the curb at the end of our road. "Yeah," he said. "They found a twenty in his pocket. He was trying to score." And with that bit of news, he ordered a round for the rest of my family and left.

The word solstice comes from the Latin *sol* ("sun") and *sistere* ("to stand still"). The two annual solstices occur when the sun appears to stall at the most northerly and southerly points in the sky. In Ireland, on the evening of the summer solstice, people spill from the pubs out onto the street. The spirits and the nighttime sun might bring music. Someone might play a guitar, or a fiddle, someone might sing. That night, as everyone trickled home after the pub, Peter and his friend rode into the city. Why? To visit a girlfriend, to buy drugs, to witness the beauty of the empty streets on this magical night of almost no darkness. He hit a curb going too fast and both boys were thrown into the trunk of a tree somewhere on the road between Finglas and Glasnevin. My brother Billy knows the exact tree. He saw the blur of lights from the back of a taxi after a drunken night out in the city. He could have stopped, he said for years after. He should have stopped. "What could you have done?" I'd ask. "I could have been with him," he'd say, "so he could have known he was not alone."

It was as if Peter was the lynchpin, and once removed, my siblings and I all spun out. Billy's girlfriend got pregnant. They announced their engagement. We were supposed to be happy for them, but we saw Billy drink pints of whiskey and start fights in Druids nightclub out the back of the Hunter's Moon. Clare got pregnant with a guy she had just started seeing, and Maria dated Peter's best friend. John slept all day and went out raving every night. Ben, a talented athlete, stopped training and started playing guitar like his brother, but instead of singing pop anthems, he spoke long improvised stream-of-consciousness song-poems about the nature of reality. Mam hid the valium stash we had all been stealing from, so I became more dependent on the whiskey to get me to the soft place, where I needed to be. Suspended between this world and that.

I slept in Peter's bed because it was the only one free. I didn't change his sheets because I didn't mind mingling with his smell, his stray hairs, his particles of skin. The days bled into one another. In the neighbor's garden, I watched Mrs. McMullen hang her washing on the line. Mrs. Byrne walked by the front carrying a bag from Centra supermarket. An airplane flew overhead. It is an uncanny thing because consciously you know people are going about their day, but subconsciously you wonder how they are able to, given the recent news. You move in different registers. Their world is still turning and yours has stopped.

David mailed care packages from New York: Keith Haring fridge magnets, a journal, pencils, love

letters, socks, and bars of my favorite candy, PayDay. One envelope had a stamp commemorating the 1997 Pathfinder Mission to Mars. I contemplated the recent discovery that seventy-four per cent of the universe is made up of dark energy. It pushes the universe out at an accelerated rate, causing time to speed up and space to expand.

After six weeks, I returned to New York, where I had trouble conforming to my former mold. I did not want to check out the great new restaurant or try the great new cocktail at the great new bar. I did not want to go to the movies or to museums. I did not want to pick out new bed linens, or smile smugly over the

New York Times on Sunday afternoons. It was clear to me that things were over with David when he called from the supermarket to ask if I wanted linguine or fettuccine for dinner. How could I respond? I could not fathom, with everything going on in my mind, how he could possibly expect me to make space for such a preposterous question.

I wanted to know, when people asked me how many kids were in my family, if I should say eight, as I had always done, or seven. But if Peter was included, then what about Michelle, our sister who died right before I was born? What about her? She had existed for me as an idea, but Peter's death somehow made her real. She lived and breathed. She had personality and an accent. So should I say "Nine, but two are dead"? That's a door to open. I might burst into tears, or worse, I might pretend like I was not bothered in order to spare any discomfort. I should just say seven, and avoid that whole dead conversation.

I tried to stay in the relationship with David for as long as I could, but in the wake of Peter's death, everything good that had been expanding between us receded into a black hole in the center of my mind through which nothing, not even light, could pass.

David had known some measure of suffering in his life, but not enough to meet me where I was. He seemed a stranger to me then, bobbing about on the surface of things. I wanted to leave. He told me I was grieving, and that it would pass. He wept and I stared back at him. Time passed, he pleaded, more time, he begged, but I was in the depths and could not reach the kind hand he extended to me.

Anyway, life had lost its meaning and planning any kind of future seemed futile. I wanted to be out living every day as if it were my last. I wanted to drink the way I wanted to and come and go as I pleased. Peter visited in my dreams. He did not seem happy, he did not seem sad, he did not seem to miss us. I'd ask him, "What's it like being dead?" He'd shrug and say, "It's OK."

There was a string of men then. It was always the same relationship and I always allowed myself to think the problem was with them: they were emotionally immature; they were afraid of commitment. Yet, for all the flaws I projected onto them, I clung to them and hated for them to leave. I'd spend my days obsessing over some comment they might have made in passing. Discussing it with anyone who would listen. Calling ten friends until someone finally said what I wanted to hear. I was always hungover and anxious, until the evening when I met up with whatever guy, ordered a drink, made a joke, and everything was OK again, at least for a couple of hours.

And so I went on for another decade before landing, finally, in sobriety.

Somewhere on the six-hour transatlantic flight to Dublin you lose five hours. Time speeds up, slows down, rolls forward, bends back, expands, contracts, and collapses in on itself. At Dublin Airport, my father is always there to pick me up. This is our ritual, his and mine: when giving my flight details, I always say, "I arrive very early in the morning, so I'll take a taxi to the house." Dad always says, "No-no! I'll be there." Only that one time, when I flew home for Peter's funeral, did I not immediately find his face in the crowd. An old man approached as I exited the arrivals gate. I looked at him a long moment before my father's presence finally registered itself. Every time since, the memory of that encounter flickers across my mind, and colors, for better or worse, the present reunion.

Even now, certain combinations of light and air on June days sink me. The body remembers what the mind cannot. Sometimes I can smell the sadness coming. Sometimes it is triggered suddenly, in surprising and unrelated ways: exiting the train at the Jay Street–MetroTech station that one time, or entering the spice shop on Atlantic Avenue another. Sometimes the sadness sticks until I remember that one does not recover from a brother's death. The stages of grief do not apply here. No sense in forcing them. There is no reconstituting our original shape. We are no better or worse than we might have been, only irrevocably, internally altered.

Anne Carson kept her notebook for ten years after her brother's death. She writes that the word *history* has its roots in the ancient Greek verb that means *to ask*. "It is when you are asking about something that you realize you yourself have survived it, and so you must carry it, or fashion it into a thing that carries itself." So on the summer solstice, I get out the box containing a photograph of Peter, a bracelet he found and gave me, a letter he wrote, but never mailed; I take Anne Carson's *Nox* from the shelf. This is my ritual: I lay the relics out and open the book. I read it cover to cover and remember it a little differently every year. Carson's strange history carries itself, and it carries me. In the reading and re-reading, I find I am not alone. I see that I have indeed survived, and that I go on, one foot in front of the other, in step with a brother who goes on beside me.

July
Blood Humors

The sky's eyes are blue, September Eleven Blue,
but not the one for now,
we are climbing the stairs in Arnotts, and I am
staring at the mother's feet.
She has had a pedicure, and her toes shimmer in
jewel-studded white sandals.
There is a blue wall, it is the blue of Mexico. I
imagine, as I have never been.

I think of my friend Hailey and wonder if she
ever felt this blue,
before the bus ripped her leg off on Canal Street
and all her blood spilled out of her...
One life, not three thousand, two months later.

We are going for coffee on the patio. I find seats
while the mother gets cappuccinos.

I hope she hurries because I am struggling with an
impulse to pitch myself over the rail
and onto Henry Street.

It is chilly outside, but we want to smoke.
Who would have thought Ireland would come to this?
The mother is only glad her father did not live to see
the day
a person would be forced to smoke a cigarette outside
in the rain and the cold.

I want to tell the mother about Hailey, but it will
make her sad.
So we talk about the price of pedicures in New York
and Dublin.
New York is cheaper. Considerably.

The last time I saw Hailey Mary Blue, all the
Haileyness had gone out of her.
Her old Vietnamese mother was crying over the
hard, white mask of a stranger
almost the same, but not quite.
It had never occurred to me, over cocktails and
cappuccinos,

over talk of boys and shoes, that Hailey had a
mother.

The mother is talking to me now. About this
and that.
I am trying to imagine being in her body. How
small she is, like a little bird.
I nod occasionally while trying to find something
familiar in her face, but she is gone,
left long ago, two of her children dead, and
almost a third, twice.

Blood from the brother's ripped wrist spurts out
like a fountain.
Spurts out like a fountain. No. *Cruor emicat, ut
fons* over the white walls of our hallway.
The father calls out for white towels, logic having
left us, I could only find red and blue.

At the hospital in Navan, the Virgin of Guadalupe
is there to welcome us.
The chalky white hollow of a cheap statue where
a hand should have been.

A hand severed from the wrist is a hand in
name only.

Years of dust had clogged her irises and fallen
in a stream to her feet,
where it settled between her toes to comfort
strangers.

Part Three
Lughnasadh

How do the living lie with the dead? Until the dehumanization of society by capitalism, all the living awaited the experience of the dead. It was their ultimate future. By themselves the living were incomplete. Thus living and dead were interdependent. Always. Only a uniquely modern form of egotism has broken this interdependence. With disastrous results for the living, who now think of the dead as eliminated.

—John Berger

August
The Great Hunger

There was, then, nothing solid inside myself, so I blew about the place, rootless and aimless. I didn't mind being a resident alien; at least the status matched how I felt. After the obligatory period, I could, if I wished, apply for US citizenship, but I was neither ready to commit, nor was I ready to go back to Ireland, not because I did not want to stay, but because there was a gap between the language and the experience of becoming an American. A distance between what I was supposed to feel about it and what I felt, a dissonance really, between the head and the gut.

I did not lay blame for my problems at the door of America. Why, after all, had I fled to her seven years prior with less than a month's rent and two suitcases of seasonally unsuitable clothes? No, what irked me was unconscious and increasingly agitated. In his late years, Carl Jung came to the conclusion that some personal disturbances may be attributed to unresolved ancestral issues. While they manifest in individuals, they are in fact unresolved problems of a collective nature. There was something before and beyond me that needed to be acknowledged and this was the time it chose to rise.

Brian and I were propping up the bar at Milano's, one of the few remaining with a reliable four a.m. closing time. We often met there after our restaurant gigs before cabbing back to Red Hook together. The Irish bartender had seen me in every sloppy state, and other than the fact that we originated from the same country, we had little in common. Her hair was short, her clothes comfortable, and she looked you in the eye and nodded (imperceptibly) by way of a greeting. She brought your drink then returned to her seat by the window to smoke and stare out at the traffic passing on Houston Street. I appreciated her lack of forced friendliness because, by that point, I didn't have the energy to reciprocate. I also appreciated her lack of interest in my, or anyone else's life; you could be anonymous in Milano's, and I expect there are still punters who are comforted by the low, red light, the gentle hum of conversation, the lonely songs on the jukebox, and the ragged faces all around.

"I am twenty-seven years old, and I don't know what I'm doing here," I told Brian. "We have just elected George Bush to be president. I really don't feel good about the future." He slugged back the dregs of his vodka-cran, half listening to me, half listening to Joni Mitchell. "I suppose I'm a bit lost and soul-sick at the moment, but I can't think of a good reason to stay. Maybe it's time to move back to Ireland." I blabbered on about the unprecedented economic boom and the incentives for returning emigrants.

"Yeah, OK," he replied, cutting me off. "So, like, America is fucked-up, Carmel, but it's where you live. Running away from it won't fix your soul. I mean..." He rolled his eyes. "We should go on a road trip, see some of the rest of the country, that'll help you make up your mind."

"A road trip, right, because that wouldn't be running away."

"Au contraire, my friend!" he said, now fully committed to the idea. "A road trip is just what is needed to reignite the core and central spark of our souls!"

"You are absolutely right, Bri," I nodded along, "but the unfortunate fact is, we haven't a fuckin' bean between us."

"Don't worry about that," he said, with the confidence of an All-American-Blue-Eyed-Boy, "the universe will provide!"

He rooted out a sketchbook and pen from his JanSport backpack, and amid the drawings of geometric shapes and body parts, penises mostly, he scrawled some equation by which he deduced we would each have to save fifteen hundred dollars to begin our trip. We would have to work along the way, he said, and we had better leave soon because, seriously, if we overthought it, we would never go.

Many bright and brilliant plans dreamed up late-night at Milano's evaporated by morning, but this one stuck around. I filled out the application for citizenship and ordered the accompanying booklet for the American History part of the exam. I intended to study while acquainting myself with this country I might one day call home. By the end of December, Brian and I had what we needed to spend at least some of the first year of the new millennium exploring the America we found ourselves in.

* * *

Old snow caked the curbs on the morning we left New York. It was early January 2001, and we took the bright rainbow above to be a positive omen. For a month we dried out at Brian's folks' place, a retirement community in Fort Myers, Florida. We let the heat penetrate our bones as we rested on the beach; drifting in and out of sleep, we made a pact to let the universe dictate our course. There would be no pushing or pulling. We would tread lightly. We would accept all gifts, and we would be grateful. In the evenings, we sat in the jacuzzi and chatted with the elders. Brian's folks fed us, made us laugh, and gave us a shimmering aqua-green 1978 Cadillac Sedan de Ville for the rest of our journey.

First stop, Key West at the end of Highway 1, the final inhabited island of the Florida Keys at the very southernmost tip of the landmass of the continental United States. The archipelago bends its elegant back along the Florida Straits where the Atlantic Ocean and the Gulf of Mexico meet, and as we drove away from the mainland, we felt ourselves leaving civilization, with all its expectations and demands. The ribbon of road unfurled before us, and the air thinned as we passed through a veil of sea-spray and sky.

Brian found a listing for a room to rent in the local paper. A bony, shirtless man answered the door. His hair and beard were long, and there was an old red parrot perched on his shoulder. His young German wife stood next to him, holding their little boy. There was something strange and familiar about her: the slight frame, the wide-set eyes, the small mouth, the dark, shoulder-length hair. I recognized, suddenly, when everyone was looking at me, that she and I were the mirror image of each other. Doppelgängers, doubles, reflections, ghosts.

I got a waitressing gig at the Fat Tuesday on Duval Street. They hired seasonal staff for Spring Break when thousands of college kids descended on the Sunshine State. Every night, I watched groups of sorority sisters vie in competitions to put condoms on bananas with their mouths. One anxious freshman got so hammered on Jell-O shots that she allowed a leather-faced local drunk to lick whipped cream off her nipples while her classmates laughed and took photos with their disposable cameras.

Brian liked to hang out at the clothing-optional pool at the Atlantic Shores Motel. He sketched the naked bodies and sold the drawings at the sunset festival held

nightly at Mallory Square. He met a couple from South Dakota. The older of the two came late to his sexuality, attempting two marriages and having a couple of kids before he could acknowledge who he was. He was so grateful, he said, to live in a time when a group of men could sit around and be naked and gay in a public place together. He mentioned to Brian, in passing, that we could stay at his family's house on Lake Okoboji in Iowa if our travels took us that way.

Every time we passed state lines the landscape changed and the energy shifted. Georgia, with her grand old plantation homes visible from the highways. Her lush lawns of green that swept down to stout peach and pecan trees that would swell with fruit in the coming seasons. This gentility and abundance existed alongside, and created, its own kind of desperate poverty. Historical and intergenerational. Ghosts of the South sang silently through the Spanish moss in South Carolina, songs that haunted the earth on which the cattle grazed, and made mirages on the long stretches of lonely road.

Dolly Parton kept us company and helped us to see the people and the places. We made a pilgrimage to her homeland and camped a few nights in the Great

Smoky Mountains. We hiked through swarms of mosquitos and watched the mists rise and roll over the dense foliage. The rains came hard, and we wondered if they would be followed by locusts, or frogs, or fiery hail. In the morning, over a paper map and a plate of pancakes in the KOA cabin, we charted a loose course for the next leg of our journey: Nashville, Saint Louis, Wichita, Omaha, Sioux City.

Leaving Tennessee, we drove into the path of a tornado. Brian pulled over and we took shelter at a roadside truck-stop. Inside, we found other travelers had done the same. Momentarily stranded, we allowed an unexpected festivity to break through. Amid the chatter, the country music got louder and more drinks were poured. After a few, Brian and I made our way, a little unsteadily, across the parking lot to the motel next door. The wind whipped about in the gathering dark, and we marveled at the heavy clouds that pressed themselves like great, pregnant bellies down to the earth. There was an electric charge in the atmosphere that was compounded by the free-wheeling feeling of traveling on the open road. Suddenly, I felt totally alone. Alone, alone. Brian had a partner, a dog, a cat, and a brother back in Brooklyn. He had family in

New Jersey. He had a college degree and a reservoir of confidence in himself. My family was four thousand miles away. I was not connected in any meaningful way to anyone or anything. I was not connected to my past or present. I had nothing, and I had nothing to lose—I could disintegrate, disappear—the danger, aliveness and violence of the moment crashed in on me, and I howled with drunken laughter into the screaming wind.

Grandfather, Great Spirit, you have been always,
and before you nothing has been,
there is no one to pray to but you.
The star nations all over the heavens are yours,
and yours are the grasses of the earth.
You are older than all need, older than all pain
and prayer.

—Dakota Prayer

In the Great Plains, a different song sailed on the wild wind that swept through the prairies. I heard it in the place names: Topeka, Keokuk, Osceola, Anoka. I saw a sign for a motel that offered free breakfast at the casino across the street. Our funds were dwindling rapidly, and we should have been staying in campgrounds, but this place was cheap, and the free breakfast made the deal worthwhile.

Bluff Casino was full at nine a.m. on a Tuesday morning. Inside, it was loud and bright: slot machines, patterned walls and carpets, blinking neon lights. The patrons were elder folk mostly, drinking coffee or beer and smoking cigarettes. Brian and I were hungover and snappish. To our dismay, there was an infinite line for the breakfast buffet. To get the free meal, you had to sign up for casino membership. We gave fake names and addresses, but the wait, the wet eggs, the weak coffee, the noise, the lights, the hangover-induced feeling of impending doom weighed us down. And with our bellies full because our hearts had sunk into them, we left for Iowa.

The house on Lake Okoboji was mid-century modern, with a great bay window overlooking the lake, wall-to-wall carpeting, milk glass, and little magazine racks that held old copies of the *New Yorker* and *Reader's Digest*. Brian and I slept in the airless children's rooms. Pink for the girl. Blue for the boy. We woke early most mornings and made eggs and coffee. We sat on the deck among the old oak trees and looked out at the other mid-century houses surrounding the lake. We wondered at this crumbling American dream, and our myriad connections to, and alienations from it.

I got a waitressing gig at the Four Seasons Bar and Restaurant. It was the main local joint, and it reminded me of one of the pubs back in Ashbourne, where multiple generations of families hung out together and drank and ate and fought and laughed and got in each other's business. Here, everyone knew everyone, and they knew I would be leaving soon, so they were free to tell me things. They told me about the abortions and the husbands who beat them. They told me the unforgivable words spoken by their father, and of the child who died in the car on the two-hour drive to the hospital in a snowstorm. They told me about the secret debt and the secret obsessions. About the anorexia and the bulimia. The Xanax and the pot. The concealed desires and dreams to one day leave this stifling place, to start over somewhere new, to start fresh, to be born again.

They came in during lunch hour and ordered a "quick snap": a shot of vodka to warm them up, to cool them down, to take the edge off. Sometimes, after a couple too many, the old guy from the go-cart track would yell at me, "You foreigner! Comin' here, stealin' our jobs!"

"Another quick snap?" I'd offer, holding up the bottle.

"Yes please," he'd respond, "Carmel, dear."

The industrial ghost towns, the late spring rain, the wide, low skies. The old sadness rising. An excess of black bile, they used to say, made the melancholic personality. Freud said mourning and melancholia are akin in that they are both responses to loss. Mourning is a conscious and healthy response to the loss of a love object. Melancholia is more complicated. It operates on the subconscious level. All the feelings of loss are present, but for what? The melancholic cannot say. This, Freud says, is a pathology.

On my days off, I sat immobile in front of the bay window and stared out at the agitated lake. The grey water, the grey sky and me a mass of atoms dispersed among them. Sometimes I wrote about the places I had seen and the people I had met. A kind of record-keeping that often grew into an unstructured essay or a short story. It was a pleasure to feel thoughts flower on the page and to experience the channeling of ideas through my body. Other times I studied my American History booklet. Among the war stories and the glory was the occasional mention of the indigenous peoples and the enslaved Africans. And while I had fuzzy feelings for the Founding Fathers and their victory over the English, I could not reconcile the fact that they continued the brutal path of colonization and the savage practice of slavery. A chasm grew between what I was being asked to accept and what the land was saying.

Brian spent his days painting the local landscapes. He said he felt something rising in the soil. The ghosts followed him home, and he began to have nightmares. "There is a disturbance in the lake," he said, in the morning, exhausted. His corn and soybean fields became more abstract; dark shapes disrupted the neatly planted rows. "We will have to leave soon," he said, but I did not want to leave because the same ghosts were showing me things. The ways this land and mine were akin. The unsettled sadness in them, and in me.

* * *

For the first time, I found myself thinking about the Irish Famine, or the Great Famine, or the Irish Potato Famine, or *an Gorta Mór* and how we are still trying to figure out what to name it. Because to name a thing, to call it out, you have to know its weight and dimensions. This requires looking from a distance and from all angles. I couldn't see the depth or breadth of it, but out on the Great Plains, I wondered if my ancestors were trying to communicate with me. I wondered if they were trying to tell me something about that time, one hundred and fifty years, or seven generations, in the past.

In the library, I went on the internet. Details about the Famine (1845–52) were becoming available to us for the first time. Ship's logs. Parliamentary Debates. Estate Diaries. Poor, Irish tenant farmers paid rent to British landlords on their own families' ancestral lands. The laws were tipped in the landlord's favor, so evictions were common. The landed gentry received an annual stipend from the British crown. If they chose to farm, the land was worked by a class of farm laborer. Having been displaced by the English colonizers, these laborers traveled the Irish country-side looking for work. During the famine years on that fertile little island, they tended the sheep, and milked the cows, and cut and baled the hay, and slaughtered the pigs, and plucked the chickens, and churned the butter, and spun the flax, and loaded the carts with the fruits of their labor for shipment, under military guard, to Britain. All the while, almost a quarter of the population of Ireland, including my paternal ancestors, either emigrated or starved to death. The *Cork Examiner* reported on December 18, 1846:

> Disease, and death in every quarter—the once hardy population worn away to emaciated skeletons—fever, dropsy, diarrhea, and famine rotting in every filthy hovel, and sweeping away of whole families ... seventy-five tenants ejected here, and a whole village in the last stage of destitution there ... dead bodies of children flung into holes hastily scratched in the earth without shroud or coffin ... every field becoming a grave, and the land a wilderness.

During the parliamentary debates of 1846, Prince Adolphus, the Duke of Cambridge, voiced the attitude of the English toward the Irish: they were subhuman, animal, savage. His suggestion to end the approaching hunger was to let them eat grass: "I understand that rotten potatoes and seaweed or even grass properly mixed, afford a very wholesome and nutritious food. We all know that Irishmen can live upon anything, and there is plenty of grass in the fields even if the potato crop should fail."

The laissez-faire economics of the day prevented the government from "interfering." Sir Charles Trevelyan, Assistant Secretary to the Treasury in charge of famine policy, is remembered in England as being a gifted civil servant. In the Irish history of Ireland, he is remembered as one of the most hated characters of British imperialism. In an 1846 letter to the Chairman of the Board of Works in Ireland, Colonel Jones, he wrote:

> Famine is a mechanism for reducing surplus population. The judgment of God sent the calamity to teach the Irish a lesson, that calamity must not be too much mitigated … The real evil with which we have to contend is not the physical evil of the famine, but the moral evil of the selfish, perverse and turbulent character of the people.

People who began planting with the goddess Brigid in February and reaping with the god of harvest, Lugh, in August, as their ancestors had done. People who told stories of such depth and variety that today the National Archives house the largest folklore collection in the world. People who drank and danced and lamented their dead for days. People who saw ghosts, and feared God, and spoke the most ancient language in Europe. That they did not respect the laws imported by English civil servants was what made them, in the eyes of the English, morally evil, selfish, perverse, and turbulent of character. God brought the potato blight to Ireland, the old ones say, but the English brought the famine.

As an Irish immigrant in America, I inhabit a strained space. Ireland was occupied by the English for centuries, and eventually became the colonial laboratory of the British Empire. Generations of Irish people fled to America, and while stories of struggle and resilience abound, there are also less-told stories of their troubled assimilation in another colonized country. One horrific example is the New York Draft Riots of 1863, when the working-class poor of the city, mostly Irish immigrants living in overcrowded tenements, revolted against the draft that required the men to sign up for the ongoing civil war. The Emancipation Proclamation had been signed earlier that year, and formerly enslaved people were making their way north to make a new life. Black men were not considered citizens, so they could not be drafted. The North had been bombarded with years of media propaganda warning against the dangers of racial intermingling. The Irish feared that if they were away fighting a war, their longshoreman and factory jobs would be taken by their new Black neighbors. During almost a week of rioting, our desperately poor Irish ancestors beat other desperately poor people to death in the streets, wrecking the places where they congregated, even burning down an orphanage for Black children.

They lynched and burned Black men and brutally beat women and children.

They savagely killed a seven-year-old boy.

Meanwhile, wealthier Americans did not have to concern themselves with the draft or fighting in the streets. They could simply pay a poor person to be drafted in their stead.

The Anglo-Irish and Irish Protestants did not get involved in the Draft Riots. It was not their fight, they were not culturally despised like their papist counterparts, but some of these Irish people had plenty invested in slavery and genocide, and there are many others who did plenty of damage just passing through.

Just after the Famine, the Anglo-Irish baronet, Sir St. George Gore, led a three-year bison-hunting expedition through the Great Plains. He had been born into an aristocratic family in County Donegal, and he is remembered in the Great Plains as one of the most notorious hunters ever to come through the lands. Even in the depths of the wilderness he demanded a strict adherence to social order. His large tent was lined with fine linens. The earth beneath it was covered with French carpets. He hired men to carry his wood-burning stove, his brass bed, his toilet, and bathtub. All the trappings, if you like, of a civilized life. He dined alone and he read Shakespeare after. He drank whiskey. He drank too much. He ran around naked and screaming. He fought with the men. He fired his gun and threatened their lives.

He left in his wake thousands of dead bison, bear, elk, and countless smaller animals. Whereas the indigenous people used every part of the kill for food, clothing, shelter, medicine, toys, tools, shoes, and rituals, the sportsmen sometimes took pelts to trade, and occasionally a head for a trophy, but often left entire animals to rot where they lay. Erasing, as it were, an ecosystem, a way of life that had existed for millennia before they arrived.

This is not what we learned in school. These are not the stories remembered on St. Patrick's Day. I tried to push it all away from myself, and yet it moved through my body. The black bile rose. Lost and soul-sick, I tried to locate myself in history but could not. In my mind, I looked to Ireland to get a sense of who I was, and the face I saw did not reflect my own, or it did, but only in faint and fading fragments. As I was hanging out in Iowa, contemplating this history, the Celtic Tiger was roaring. A zealous building boom drove the economy, and the land churned up the bones of the dead, the mass unmarked graves of the Famine-Genocide.

Late-night at the Karaoke Lounge, red and blue strobes lit a makeshift stage. The old man behind the bar turned a dirty rag around a thick glass ashtray. He raised his expressionless hound-dog face to Tammy, my waitress friend from another restaurant, as she did that Patsy Cline song for the three lone customers: old men in checkered shirts and trucker caps. Brian also liked to belt out a tune. Dressed in Nikes, ripped jeans, and a pink T-shirt, he leapt about the stage, doing that Violent Femmes number for the same audience.

We arrived back in New York in late August, 2001. For a few weeks, I stayed with my friend Robert on the Lower East Side, because by the grace of the great spirit, his roommate was away touring with his band. I offered to help Robert paint the apartment by way of thanks for letting me stay. We carefully removed all the Mexican and religious art from his walls, the symbols that honored his family's heritage. We taped the corners and covered the furniture with plastic. By the end of the day, we were exhausted, so we ordered Chinese food and rented the movie *American Beauty* from the Blockbuster on Houston Street.

In the morning, I heard Robert run out of his bedroom. He called down the hall, "Did you hear that?" He went into the living room and turned on the TV news.

"Hey love," he called, "you better come out here."

In the half-sleep before the world has had a chance to assemble itself, we watched in confusion, a few neighborhoods over, the smoke, the people jumping from the towers, the blue American sky. The second plane.

The phones did not work, and the bridges and tunnels were closed, so we walked around the neighborhood watching the ghostly droves trudge north. People covered in white dust: their business suits, their shoes, their hair, their lashes, the skin around their wide and wet eyes. Emergency vehicles speeding, sirens blaring. We did not know what was happening and we did not know what to do, but somehow, by early evening, we found our way to Botanica Bar on East Houston Street. There was no power, so we lit candles and sat outside on the stoop to let passersby know that if they needed a place, this one was open. But the great grey cloud enveloped us, and we could not be seen.

We sought out each other's eyes because all the protective barriers the city teaches us to erect had crumbled. We were, for a moment, liberated from the burden of our individual concerns. We were not connected by race or class or nationality or gender or sex or any qualifying identity marker, but by something deeper. The realization that I am you, and we are…

That state passed quickly, and the small self returned, kicking and screaming in terror. "I feel like

I am about to be blown up at any moment," I told Robert. He felt the same. We went in search of our life-tools: his, a Jameson, neat; mine, a vodka tonic. Our plan of action was to attain and maintain a state of comfortable numbness until all the drama passed. *We are inhaling the dust of the dead*, we said, and we drank. *This might be our last night on earth*, we said, and we drank. Tense and expectant on the edge of another explosion, we reached out shaking hands, picked up our glasses, and drank.

We hit the bars that were open in the East Village. We did a tour and ended the night in Robert's local gay bar, the Boiler Room, watching CNN and doing shots until we couldn't walk. We wobbled back to his place on Attorney Street, but when we were stopped by the Army and asked for ID to re-enter, the closeness of the tragedy hit upon us, and we both broke down. Messy and emotional, we clung to each other and sobbed all night long.

The next night I walked through the neighborhood alone. The cloud, now roux-colored, had thickened and covered the whole of downtown. It was not possible to see more than a few feet ahead. Pictures of the missing began to appear: mothers and fathers, brothers and sisters, children and friends. The missing would not be buried according to the rites of their people. They would not be taken back to the place of their birth and interred in the earth, or scattered on the land of their natal home. They would go without the rituals that have evolved with us to give death the sliver of meaning that enables the living to go on.

A lone saxophonist stood at the corner of Houston and Crosby. He played Miles Davis's *Blue in Green*. The notes hung heavy and low in the thick air. As I passed, I stopped a moment and found his eyes, a sort of prayer, to let this St. Francis know I could see him preaching to the birds, saying all of the unsayable things with the immediacy of music for the odd straggler like me, and for the multitude of souls leaving this earth.

Overnight, the world changed. The Global War on Terrorism began. A month after September 11, I caught the train and a bus out to a facility in Queens to take my citizenship test. All of us from all over the world arrived with our study booklets and our stories. Some were in groups; others were alone, like me. As we checked in, I looked around; a large number would have to relinquish their native citizenship in order to become American. Being Irish, I gratefully did not have to make that decision.

Little cubicles divided the giant warehouse-like space. Even though I had studied, I was still anxious about the US History and Government test. I took my seat across from the uniformed immigration officer, a young man with a square jaw and a crew cut.

"Nervous?" he asked.

"Yes," I smiled.

"Are you ready?" he asked.

I sat upright in the chair. "I am."

"Who is the president of the United States?"

A trick question? I looked at him in alarm.

"Em… George W. Bush?" I answered finally.

"Congratulations, Ms. Mc Mahon. Welcome to America!"

A little confused, I made my way toward the exit. I passed people who sobbed tears of joy, and others tears of anguish. One old woman in a hijab was in despair. Her family cried too, and tried to comfort her. Did she not know the answer was George W. Bush? More likely she had had more difficult questions, and lots of them. Her cries followed me, and a lump formed in my throat. I turned around, and if I could have in that moment, I would have given her my result. "Here, take it, I don't want it." But it doesn't work that way. I worked, paid taxes, and stayed out of jail, and, while they say it is not a requirement, I had enough experience in this country to know that the privilege afforded by the time and place of my birth made me the ideal candidate for US citizenship.

I became a citizen the following month. I swore allegiance at a Brooklyn courthouse in a room with murals from the 1930s depicting lazy natives and virtuous, hardworking pilgrims. Outside, family members rushed up, joyfully hugging and kissing and congratulating the new Americans. They waved their little plastic flags. I had arranged no celebration. I stopped in at a diner for a cup of coffee and picked up my laundry on the way home.

Early in the new year, my certificate of citizenship from the White House arrived in the mail. It was accompanied by a letter that contained these beautiful lines:

Americans are united across the generations by grand and enduring ideals. The grandest of these ideals is an unfolding promise that everyone belongs, that everyone deserves a chance, and that no insignificant person was ever born. Our country has never been united by blood or birth or soil. We are bound by principles that move us beyond our backgrounds, lift us above our interests, and teach us what it means to be citizens.

And as the fighter planes bulleted the blue skies over Afghanistan, our forty-third president, George W. Bush, signed the letter welcoming me into the arms of America.

In the summer of 2002, Robert and I moved into a place in Chinatown. It was an old loft that used to be a sweatshop. The landlord knew we lived there, even though the lease said we were not allowed to. It was freezing in winter and boiling in summer, but the rent was cheap, and it was perfect. I was to begin at the School of Continuing and Professional Studies at NYU that fall. I promised myself I would cut down on the drinking by then. School was a pleasure, but it did nothing to curtail my deepening alcoholism. After a year, I discovered that, even with all the scholarships and fellowships, there was no way I was going be able to pay for NYU. I transferred to the City College and found a kind of home there among the immigrants and students of Harlem. I continued my study of English with a focus on women's and postcolonial writing, even as the corners of my sanity were beginning to split and fray.

I discovered the work of Maeve Brennan. She was a young Irish immigrant who became a staff writer at the *New Yorker* before the disease of alcoholism colonized her life. It took her marriage, her job, and her home, and it left her dragging her cats and bags around the midtown streets, sneaking in to sleep or bathe in the restrooms at the *New Yorker*. She died in a nursing home in Queens ten days before I arrived in 1993. I thought of her often in those days and wondered how many more Irish women might have lived their lives out this way. Might I disappear with them, the unrevived, the disconnected and forgotten?

By the time I finished college, I was drinking every day. Which included the days I did not want to drink. I got a job as an office assistant at the Whitney Museum of American Art and, walking home in the evening, I would try to pass the liquor store, but my feet of their own accord would walk right in. I would watch my hand, as if it belonged to someone else, reach up and lift a bottle from the shelf. Shocked at midnight that I had lost four hours, and shocked again at four that I had lost another four. Where had the hours gone? Where had I been?

In a daze, I'd sometimes wander down to Battery Park City to where the Irish Hunger Memorial sits amid the buildings of high finance. The memorial was being built when the Twin Towers fell next door. It was co-designed by the American artist Brian Tolle, and it includes the ruin of a nineteenth-century Irish cottage from County Mayo, the bones of a home that once housed generations of a family. The cottage was carried over the ocean and reset stone by stone in this place of commerce and yachts and chain restaurants. The missing roof and walls are sketched in with words like these. Words that reach for meaning in absences and try to make links between people and stones. The grounds are planted with the fauna and flora of North-West Ireland through which grow the familiar clusters of clover, buttercup, dandelion and daisy.

The entire area is a manmade infill that was laid in the early 1970s from rock excavated during the construction of the World Trade Center. I'd sit under the absence of the Twin Towers and watch young finance women and men pass by. Blue shirts. Gym bodies. You hear Irish accents on the streets of this neighborhood, the way you used to hear them passing a construction site or by the waiter's station in an Irish bar. How far we've come, I'd think, the descendants of ignorant, starving savages.

That place and its sediment of stories. Why keep dragging the past into the present? Because back then, I pushed it down until my thoughts became dark and chaotic; until voices emerged telling me that if I were to end my life, no one would really miss me. Sure, they would be upset for a while, but they'd get over it, in time. For so long I had been rootless and aimless, a hungry ghost. In ancient Ireland, it was a fate worse than death to be ousted from your *tuatha* or tribe. Without the connections that reflected who you were, you ceased to exist.

I was trying to connect to something. There were popular narratives of the Irish in America, but I couldn't quite make them fit with the facts. America, a country that was never united by blood or birth or soil, imposes itself violently on nations that are. And so I began to ask the question, is it pathological to mourn for your ancestors, and the ancestors in the soil on which you stand? Or is it pathological to pretend they are not there, not *here*, with us now?

It takes a long time, after you stop drinking, for the fog to lift. In 2016, I went with a sober friend to see the Brontë papers at the Morgan Library. Patrick Brunty was an immigrant from Ireland. In England, he changed his name to what he considered the more refined Brontë. Even though the family was Protestant, to their English neighbors they were still Irish, and so inferior: they were outsiders, bizarre Celts, a big red-headed man with his *tuatha* of bold, bad-humored children. Tuberculosis decimated most of the family, but not before three of the greatest novels in English literature were published by Charlotte, Emily, and Anne, and all in the darkest year of the Irish Famine, "Black '47."

The writer and critic Terry Eagleton was born in England to Irish parents. He suggests that the character of Heathcliff from Emily's *Wuthering Heights* may have been based on the young famine waifs crowding into the streets of Liverpool in the early 1840s. It is possible that on his visits there, her brother Branwell may have seen these kids and reported their appearance back at Haworth. Eagleton says of the scene where Heathcliff meets the Earnshaws for the first time:

> Earnshaw unwraps his greatcoat to reveal to his family a 'dirty, ragged, black-haired child' who speaks a kind of 'gibberish', and who will later be variously labeled beast, savage, demon, and lunatic. It's clear that this little Caliban has a nature on which nurture will never stick, and that's merely an English way of saying that he's quite possibly Irish.

We stood before the portrait of the three famous sisters painted by Branwell. They sit pretty in the foreground, and the faint outline of Branwell stands in the back. He had included, then erased, himself. We know this guy. These antics. He was an alcoholic, and this is the perfect portrait of one: wanting to be seen and wanting to hide at the same time. Always somehow at the center of things, but fragile, apart, and alone, haunting the picture like a ghost that will disappear if looked at in the wrong way. *We see you, friend*, we tell him, because we know there are particles of him in the paper before us, and we know they are altered by our observation of them, and we know he can hear us across the distance of space and time.

In Ireland, both sides of my father's family were poor farm laborers like their County Down neighbors, the Bruntys. A whole generation of these ancestors was forced to emigrate during the Famine-Genocide. Most crossed over to Glasgow in Scotland, a thriving industrial town in the mid-nineteenth century. They crowded into tenements and were despised by the local population for being drunk and dirty and ignorant, and carrying all kinds of diseases, and all the things people still say about new immigrant populations.

One of my paternal great-grandmothers died of Bright's disease during childbirth at the age of thirty-seven, leaving four children under the age of ten. They were sent to the poorhouse, as their father could not work and take care of them. He was heart-broken and destitute. While drunk, he signed up with the British Army. My family spits his shamed name, Laurence Bradley. He became a Colliery Pithead Sapper in the Royal Engineers, and he was, less than a month after the Easter Rising in Ireland, blown to smithereens over Flanders Fields. Here is the triumph of colonialism: you can destroy the soul of a people; you can take their land and their resources; you can make their children cogs in your machine; and even as they are rising up against you, some of their own will be laying down their lives in your name.

I have done mortifying things while drunk. There have been foggy mornings where I imagined all was well before an image from the night before flashed across my mind. *Did I dream it?* I ask myself, scrambling to brush the strokes of memory back into a coherent image. I wonder if it was so for Laurence Bradley, coming to with a "King's Shilling" in his hand? Or was it his intention all along, a suicide mission, to escape the overwhelm, oppression, trauma, and grief of his short life?

His daughter, my grandmother, Elizabeth, at age fourteen, was sent alone by train to Paisley to work in service at the Gardiner residence, a wealthy family in the town. She shook in terror for the entire journey, for she had heard what happened to young orphan girls with no one to protect them. She had heard about the masters and the sons and how they took what they pleased, and about the mistresses who looked the other way.

Lizzie worked her way up from scullery maid to parlor maid. Her mistress was a kind woman who brought her tokens from her travels: an ivory-inlaid box from India, a delicate wallet of red leather from Morocco. Mrs. Gardiner converted to Catholicism and through the Church she made an introduction between Lizzie and her future husband, Willie Mc Mahon. While Lizzie knew how very lucky she had been, she always said her life began at the age of twenty-eight, the day she married my grandfather.

Months before her wedding in 1929, Lizzie's younger brother, George Toner Bradley, at age twenty-five, boarded the SS *Cameronia* in Glasgow and set off for New York City. I watch YouTube videos of recently colorized film of New York in the 1920s, and I am struck by how similar it looks. The same streets with their recognizable buildings and landmarks: the Flatiron, the old lamp posts, the railings at Central Park. George landed in Ellis Island, and no one ever heard from him again. Where did he go? Was he turned back? Was his name changed? Did he start a new life elsewhere? Did he get into iron work, his family trade back home? Did he watch the people jump from the towers of high finance when the stock market crashed five months after he arrived? Did he get involved in the gangs that ruled the city? Did he die anonymous and alone on the streets of New York? Lizzie worried about her little brother until the day she died in 1983. A decade later, I set out for New York without so much as a thought for any of them.

Lizzie and Willy had five children. My father, the youngest, moved back to Ireland in the late 1960s where he met my mother, and they set about, they joke, replenishing the famine-decimated population. As I traced the story of my father's family, I rooted out the few photographs of them that I had collected over the years. I placed them around my desk and examined every image, looking into the eyes of the long-dead and trying to imagine their everyday lives, how they spoke and moved. What they thought, and how they loved. I began to dream about them.

The flickering images of childhood visits to Scotland returned. Like when, in the dark hours of the morning, my parents loaded us all into the Citroën Safari and we drove up past Belfast in the North of Ireland to the ferry port of Larne. Passing through the no man's land of border country, Dad shouted suddenly, "Not a bloody word!" because he had seen them from a distance. He slowed and stopped the car, and in the misty light, we watched them jump from the hedges and approach like an apparition, three uniformed British soldiers carrying guns. "Not a bloody word." Dad said again, as he rolled the window down and greeted the young men. They looked in at us, slowly. We barely breathed. I began a rosary in my head. Dad used his friendly voice and said we were just going on holiday, back to the old country. He showed them his British passport. They asked if we were all his. Seven children and a very pregnant wife. Dad made a joke and they finally waved us on. The air returned, but no one spoke for the rest of the drive. On the ferry, Mam found seats on the deck and as she sat back, in her white cotton dress, she closed her eyes and turned her face to the sun. She was smiling as we all took turns putting our heads on her belly to feel the new baby kicking. I was thinking about the soldiers and the fear in my father's voice. I wondered if they would have killed us, even Mam with a baby growing in her belly.

I continued to flesh out fragments of conversations, glimpses of interiors, forgotten feelings. Writing out toward something niggling at the periphery, I had a vague memory of being taken to Edinburgh as a child. The grey buildings, the cobblestones, the narrow streets. Why had we driven there from Paisley? I googled Edinburgh and the first results that came up were of Edinburgh Castle. Yes, I had been there before; I had seen the name of my great-grandfather listed in the logbooks from World War I. For some reason, I knew I had to visit, and see it again.

I sent an email to my French friend Valerie, asking if she'd be up for meeting me there for the weekend. I spooned some soil from Inwood Hill Park into an old medication container and packed it in my suitcase, not at all sure of how I might use it. I have come to learn that ritual is just about taking an action, so the associated thought, desire, or intention can be impressed upon the body and made into an experience.

On a cold, crisp afternoon, Valerie and I walked up the cobbled hill toward the castle, catching up, coffees in hand. Inside, I told the security woman the story of Laurence Bradley and his son, George Toner Bradley. She said that photography was not allowed, and she would be going into the next room, where she would not see me taking a picture of Laurence's name.

BOYD...
293238 Pte b. Partick Lanarkshire Died Home
10/10/1918. latterly 661578, Labour Corps.

Died F&F
h Bn Tyneside

BRADLEY, Joseph
4582 Pte b. Bridgeton Glasgow Killed in action
F&F 31/7/1917. latterly 235031, 1/4th Bn. The
Loyal North Lancashire Regt.

led in action F&
Coy , formerly

BRADLEY, Laurence
147940 Spr b. Dalziel Lanarkshire Killed in
action F&F 8/6/1916. 255th Tunnelling Coy ,
formerly S/8802, Seaforth Hldrs

BRADLEY, Thomas
400517 Pte b. Houston Killed in action F&F
29/3/19... latterly 27063, 1/7th Bn The
Durham Light Inf.

ed in action F&

d Home

BRANAGAN, Edward
425899 Spr b. Camlachie Lanarkshire Died
Egypt 4/11/1918. 357th Water Coy., formerly
8901, HLI

d in action F&f
t.

BRAND, Edward
402216 L Cpl. Killed in action F&F 21/7/1918.
401st Field Coy.

anarkshire Kill

BRAND, James
88770 S...

6174 P
F&F 1
Black

BROW
3572 I
26/9/1
North

BROW
79665
action
forme

BROW
4595
2/5/1

BRO\
1514
Kille
S/49

BRO
757:
1/10
R. S

Coming out of the castle, Valerie and I headed down the street to St. Giles' Cathedral. Founded in the twelfth century and built in the fourteenth, this structure has spent half of its life as a Catholic institution and half as a Protestant one. Inside the grand nave, tourists took photos of the impressive blue vaulted ceiling, while an enthusiastic minister tried to corral them into the pews for the evening service. Members of the faithful had been trickling in. Some sat with their heads bent amid the old stone and hushed tones, as if they had always been there, through time and change, deep in prayer and bathed in the dusty shafts of low afternoon light.

We came upon a small, unoccupied side-chapel with carved wooden panels on the walls, an empty altar and a warm wooden bench for rest and contemplation. This is the place, I told Valerie. I took the container of New York soil out of my coat pocket, held it in my hands and said a prayer for my family, the living and the dead, then slipped it behind an old pipe. I imagined the soil contained particles of my missing granduncle and in bringing it here, I hoped, at least ritually, to reunite this son with his father. Two bodies literally and figuratively erased by colonial history. I thought of the connection between Brigid, the goddess of planting, and Lugh, the god of reaping. Lugh's name invokes the oath or promise that what is planted in the earth will in time grow. And so, what is buried, secrets and stories, will in time find a way to surface and be told. Maybe this is why I went to New York, all those years ago, an unknown motive behind the escape, to heal the family haunting that had shown up in me. To see my forebears fully, and through them to draw a timeline and to see my place on it, to acknowledge their lives and their suffering, so that those who come after us can tread a little lighter not on Ireland, or England, or America, but on the earth that will hold the dust of us all.

September
A Day at a Time

My office job at the Whitney was probably one that a sober person could do with ease, but by the time I started working there, I was already in the final stages of my drinking career. I was unaware that positions of this sort, while miserably paid, are usually reserved for Ivy-educated daughters until they find a husband, not for broke Irish immigrants with anxiety and drink problems.

I liked to imagine I was maintaining a veneer of normalcy, but then I would accidentally wear my shirt inside out, or absentmindedly forward an inappropriate email to the entire staff. Most days were spent hiding behind my monitor, praying for relief from yet another banging hangover and vowing to never drink again. Worst of all, I would burst into tears for no reason, other than the fact that my unconscious mind had kicked up some mundane memory from the past, like the time I stood with school friends at dusk, in one of Ashbourne's newer housing estates; we were laughing while the dying light played red and gold notes across our faces and hair. Why the laughter? Why the pristine preservation of this isolated fragment? And why now, to feel it viscerally twenty years later? To feel this disconnected part of myself scramble to fit into this life.

So, while my behavior was never the stuff of dismissals, I sensed a talking-to was in the offing. I would never have survived the embarrassment. I knew that they knew that my mind had emigrated with a bottle of whiskey and what showed up was the derelict and disheveled body it had once inhabited. I had no choice but to quit.

I got a job as a personal assistant to a wealthy woman on the Upper East Side. It took a while for me to train her to call me her assistant rather than her secretary, and it took a while for me to learn that I was not being paid for my opinion.

The big apartment was a balm for my troubled soul. The objects arranged in it were beautiful. Beauty beyond intellect, beyond argument. My boss, a lifelong collector, had a reputation for having a great eye. She flipped through the auction house catalogs, stopping at the pieces that fit the esthetic she had cultivated from childhood; from within herself, impervious to outside influence or market tastes. She never attempted to articulate the meaning of an object, as my set did, flapping about trying to pin our opinions on air; she didn't have to. The housekeeper was a kind and gentle Haitian woman whose presence calmed every room she entered. And then there was Mlle. Georgette Moreau…

You see women like this in New York: keen-eyed and ancient with impeccable style, from the overall affect of their manner to the smallest detail of their dress. Georgette's job was Personal Stylist to my boss, a position wherein she managed my boss's wardrobe and yay'd and nay'd the offerings of French and Italian couturiers. I was fascinated. She, however, made no effort to hide the fact that she did not like the cut of my jib.

Every day I offered to make her cup of tea and every day she refused. There was a certain cup, a level for the water, the length of time a tea bag should steep. A complicated procedure. Certainly too much for a nervy, distracted people-pleaser to deal with. I could feel her eyes on me as I made endless cups of tea for myself, with last night's booze oozing through my pores, my breath thick, my hands shaking.

Six months had passed when she began to open up to me, in the form of a rant. She would unload the tale of some dissatisfaction she had encountered on the way to work. It usually began with the bus driver. He drove too fast, he drove too slow, he allowed too many people on the bus, he did not respond when she said hello. A sure sign that the end days were upon us when small civilities were so readily dispensed with. Some man at the bank, a cyclist, a traffic light, a pothole, a tourist, a dog, etc. Then for the rest of the day, all the events of her life would be filtered through the lens of that dissatisfaction. My stock response was a usually a sympathetic "Hmm, hmm," for I could certainly relate to the difficulties of existing alongside others when you are always in the right.

Whenever she mentioned wartime France, Georgette had my full attention. Those few years had shaped her, shaped her still, halfway around the world in time and space. "People did not groom their dogs in France during the war," she would say. "They did not waste their pennies on such frivolities as bows and booties for their pets, they did not bend down to pick up their shit! People who have dogs in the city are sick. Selfish, sick people!"

By Christmas, my life was in freefall. I was not paying my bills, or returning phone calls, or opening my mail, but I did manage to send one Christmas card. It was to my brother Billy, who was living in Greece with his wife and son. In it I scrawled the note:

I've had the worst year of my life. Merry Christmas! Love, Carmel.

For the first time in the fifteen years since I moved to America, my brother called me.

"What's the problem?" he asked. I gave him the litany: the job, the rent, the guy, the parents, the health insurance, the weather, the government, the climate, the war, etc., etc. He said, "Why don't I come visit?"

Billy arrived in January 2009, while my roommate was on vacation. He was sober now and every line in him was different. I barely recognized him for his relaxed face and his shining eyes. Night after night he sat across from me at my kitchen table. He smoked and drank coffee. I smoked and drank whiskey. He regaled me with stories from his drinking days. The crazy things he did. We roared with laughter. Unlike him, I had never gotten fired from a job or been arrested or made homeless due to my drinking. Still, I knew what he was talking about. I knew the uptightness, the discomfort, the all-or-nothing thinking, and I assumed that, with his new gifts of perception, he had articulated some of our common family traits. After he left, all the things he said stayed with me, as if he had planted seeds in my psyche that began to grow beyond my control, breaking into my dreams and, in my waking life, making the alcohol taste sour and strange.

At work, Georgette started to accept a cup of tea. She directed me in the making of it, as the English *directrice* of her primary school had directed her. "The English," she would say, "know how to make a cup of tea." Hmm. The Irish, I happened to know, make it better, but I made no mention. She accepted a biscuit only if it was made with real sugar and real butter. These biscuits she nibbled for an achingly long time. What memories, I wondered, still lurked beneath the layers of Chanel, Vuitton, Hermès?

Georgette was eighty years old, and among other minor ailments, she developed a pain in her leg, which her doctor put down to age. It was an inconvenience because it prevented her from taking her daily walk home across Central Park. She began to limp in an exaggerated fashion to match her increasingly cantankerous moods. Some days she would drag her foot behind her and mutter curses in French and stubbornly refuse my insistent offers of help.

Increased absences forced my boss to address the situation. "Perhaps it is time to retire, Gigi?" she tentatively put forth. The following day, Georgette entered in a particularly beautiful camel-hair coat and a pale pink pashmina. Her cropped silver-grey locks were spiked, punk-style. "I know when I am not wanted!" she yelled, as she threw her keys down. "I quit!" Then she turned around and hobbled out. My heart sank. The Haitian housekeeper could not eat for days, and my boss took to her bed.

I missed the presence of the old woman telling the same stories over and over, a soothing steadiness in my fraying life. Not the words themselves because I had long ceased listening, but the surety of the cadence, of knowing how each episode would play out: the way her brother would berate her for dipping her bread in her soup—just because they were poor, did not mean they had to act like peasants. The apple tree in her mother's garden from which jams and jellies were made. There was no obesity then, she would say, because the people ate what they needed and walked because they had to.

It is hard to talk about these dark days, because they are awash in a dreamy, gauzy haze, as if I were floating through them, because to have been fully present in my body would have been much too painful. Which is to say, alcohol, my constant companion, my numbing friend, was no longer working. When I drank, nothing happened but the first niggling pulses of the hangover. If you have been to this place, you will know what it means not to want to live and not to want to die, and this, I have come to learn from my fellow drunks, is what is called the jumping-off place.

I started going to Mass at Old St. Patrick's on Mott Street. I figured it couldn't hurt, as the pain was most certainly spiritual in nature. I walked there through the brittle, black and white streets, sometimes showing up with my thrift-store trench coat thrown over my pajamas, reeking of cigarettes and booze, yesterday's makeup sliding down my face.

One Sunday, a very good-looking couple marched themselves up to the front pew. They were both tall.

He was dark haired and classically handsome, and she was a Russian model with blonde waves cresting down her back. I found them abhorrent and spent the better part of the service focused on what I perceived to be their innumerable flaws: their phoniness, their overconfidence, their perfectly symmetrical faces. After a few weeks, the man began showing up alone. One Sunday, he followed me out. "Hi!" he called after me. *What does this prick want?* I thought to myself. He invited me for coffee, and before I knew it, we were walking around the neighborhood, deli coffees in hand. Thankfully, he was a talker, so I just had to nod along.

On a bench in the basketball court on Spring Street, he proceeded to tell me, out of nowhere, the story of his drinking and his recent sobriety. I was baffled as to why he was speaking of it, because I had told no one about my struggles with alcohol. I had mentioned to a friend in passing that I thought, maybe, I might have a problem, and she suggested I just not drink so much. Excellent advice, I thought, ignorant of the illness that had me in its grip. The guy used many of the same words and phrases my brother had used, and again, I found myself in familiar territory. The penny dropped. I related to the thoughts and feelings my brother had spoken of, not because I was a Mc Mahon, but because I was a garden-variety alcoholic.

Walking home, I felt I had glimpsed something of the relationship between individual and collective consciousness, and the material conditions of the world. Somehow I understood that my arrival at this moment, in this place, in this life, was not entirely my own doing. Clarity and anger burned by turns. Enough to see that something had to be done and done now. The time had come to face myself. The next morning, I emailed the guy and asked him to take me to a meeting.

There were headaches as a result of alcohol withdrawal in those early days of sobriety, along with sweats, mood swings, and fits of tears. But also, in that strange spring, there was the elation of seeing the streets of New York burst forth with the pink candy floss of cherry blossoms. All the sweetness: the sky and the shape-shifting clouds, the children, the dogs and the tattooed dads in Columbus Park. I sipped iced coffees and watched the breeze bend the blades of grass as it rushed past, ecstatic, electric, and alive. I loved the evening meetings, and the church basements, and the smoking outside, and I especially loved the stories of people's lives. It was always the same plot structure, but each telling, through the lens of an individual consciousness, worked like a spell to waken something dormant in me. I began to lift my head and look people in the eye. The connective tissue of a smile or some small talk. At the age of thirty-six, I had been given a second chance at life, and for the first time, without the aid of alcohol, I felt all right.

Sometimes, after work and before an evening meeting, I would visit Georgette at home. She lived with a fat, furry cat in a rent-controlled apartment on the Upper West Side: doorman, marble lobby. The kind of place that New Yorkers die for. She loved having me over, and she made a show of dressing for the occasion. I also took care on those days to wear something I thought she would approve of. Usually one of my many Givenchy-inspired vintage dresses, which she would briefly admire before giving me in-depth instructions on how to deal with a tiny rip or stain in the fabric.

I brought cheese and bread. The table was always laid for tea with mismatched cups and saucers. There was always a bowl of cherries and a plate of chocolates. The teapot, she always told me, was from a flea market upstate.

Georgette spoke of her first years in the US. Of the time she worked for a young Englishwoman in Florida who had married a wealthy old man for his money; when they divorced, the woman moved to New York, bought a tiny studio on Central Park South and drank herself to death in it. Of the time she worked as a cook for Woody Allen, a sweet and simple man, she claimed, who invited her to use his apartment before she found one of her own.

More stories! I demanded, drunk on Earl Grey and Petit Écolier. I felt something with that old woman that I had not felt before in my life. It was this: that sitting in her apartment with her prattling on, and the cat, and the tea, and the evening sun, I was, in those moments, exactly where I was meant to be.

As the months turned, I became aware of the descent of Georgette's mind and body. She began to answer the door in her dressing gown. Once, she told me about her previous cat, Melou, who had passed away; she had taken the ashes into Central Park and scattered them over Strawberry Fields. I asked her when it was that Melou had died; she turned around to face a framed painting of a black and white cat. "Melou," she asked it, "when did you die?" Then she turned back to me and replied, "Fifteen years ago." After that, whenever I left, she held onto me when I hugged her goodbye, and I had the feeling that I was holding a little child. I gently rubbed her hollow, papery back and promised to return soon.

One afternoon I called Georgette's apartment to make a tea date. The phone rang and rang. A few days later I called again, and again, no answer. I went to Georgette's building, and the doorman told me that she had fallen, and had been found where she lay, babbling and incoherent in a pool of her own urine. She was taken to the hospital, and then on to a nursing home on the Upper East Side.

The lobby of the nursing home was set up with seating arrangements for guests. There were none. The receptionist barely acknowledged my presence and omitted to tell me that the elevator was out of service, so I sat on an oilcloth-covered sofa for ten minutes watching the light travel up and down but never stop on the ground floor. There was a lonely feeling. Not any

lonelier than the loneliness that is always present every-
where, but here, there was less of an effort to disguise it.
Finally, I took the stairs. Good to keep the body moving,
I thought, to console myself.

I found Georgette slowly making her way, with a
walker, down the peach-pink corridor. She was barely
recognizable. Her hair and nails were long and unkempt.
The stained green nightdress did not belong to her, and
a pair of mismatched socks bunched around her ankles.
She was so thin, but her eyes were clear and bright and
shone with a new light. We putzed on together very
slowly, and she introduced me to her new Polish friend,
a pretty young blonde aide. "I can't keep up with this
one speeding about," the blonde woman said. We small-
talked a while, and we laughed at ourselves in an easy
way, we three European women, we three rebels who
had left kith and kin to end up in this place together, on
this day in September, in this year of Our Lord.

Georgette and I walked on. "I have been here so
long," she told me, "that I have no memory of my life
outside this place." It has only been a week, I thought
to myself, but perhaps it is just as well. "My mind is
lucid for what is in front of my face and my memories
of Burgundy," she said, "but everything else is gone."

When visiting hours were over, she walked me to the door. "It's not so bad," she said. "I just take it a day at a time, and today is a very good day, because you are here..." I held her for a long time, for what I knew would be the last time, and I felt the healing begin within me of a very deep wound that I didn't even know was there.

October
On the Dark Side
of the Head

Migraines are often listed as a symptom of trauma. I had my first one at age thirty-six, a few months after I began recovery. So migraines and alcoholism are forever connected in my mind. It was as if the things that alcohol tamped down rose up and brought with them this crushing new illness. In order to stay sober, I learned, I would have to unearth the root causes and conditions of why I drank, and those causes, it turns out, are continually being revealed.

Lately, I am considering the nameless pain that doesn't seem to be rooted in my personal experience. An illness of the spirit, let's say. Ancient and ancestral. Where is the physician who can cure it? With what language can I say, "Yes, I'm here because a thousand hungry ghosts hurt inside me?" The physician, of course, is also inside me, but it seems I will only consult her when all other options have been exhausted. When

I have no other recourse but to sit down and write my way to a reconnection with those who have gone before.

In 1961, Carl Jung wrote a letter to Bill Wilson, one of the co-founders of Alcoholics Anonymous. Jung observed that in his alcoholic patients, the "craving for alcohol was equivalent on a low level, of the spiritual thirst of our being for wholeness." There was, he thought, some internal drive toward unity and connection. He found it telling that the word *spiritus* is used to describe both "the highest religious experience" and "the most depraving poison." Most alcoholics in recovery can remember their first drink, even decades later, in acute detail: where we were, what we wore, who we were with. We remember because when we ingested this substance, something profound happened to us. The nameless pain inside us temporarily abated.

In Irish, the term for whiskey is *uisce beatha*, water of life, because really, for some of us, that is what alcohol is: the thing that enables us to live, at least for a time—until it doesn't anymore. Jung's prescription for overcoming alcoholism was to fight spirits with spirit, *spiritus contra spiritum*.

In addition to the spiritual aspect of alcoholism, there is also a mental one. For over a decade, I had been either drunk or hungover, and with the progression of my disease, the hangovers consumed three full days with drink sickness: the blunt ache in the head, the nausea, the cored-out emptiness of wasted time collapsing in on my chest. I would spend that time in bed, swearing off alcohol forever. But, as soon as I began to feel the slightest bit better, the thought would arise, seemingly out of nowhere, *Maybe I'll just have one*, and once that thought broke through, there was no sending it back, it grew louder and more persistent. *Just one drink*, it demanded. *What harm?*

But alcoholism isn't only an illness of the spirit or the difficult-to-articulate realms of the mind and emotions. It is also an illness of the body. In the early days of AA, there was identified in people with alcoholism a common physical trait that they called "the phenomenon of craving." Once a person with alcoholic tendencies had a drink, they had to have another. I can see so clearly now that this is true, but when I was drinking, something prevented me from grasping the simple fact, even with over a decade's worth of evidence to the contrary, that I could never have just *one*. That some bodies might have an abnormal reaction to alcohol has been contested for many years, so a 2019 study at the Perelman School of Medicine at the University of Pennsylvania examined the biology driving recovering alcoholics to relapse. They found that acetate produced in the liver during the breakdown of alcohol travels to the brain's learning system and alters proteins that regulate DNA function. This affects our behavior, so that when we are confronted with certain environmental cues, drinkers, they found, drink.

I may have had migraines in the past that were masked by drink sickness, and there were certainly headaches as the result of alcohol withdrawal in those first foggy months of sobriety. But then this headache arrived, so I took a Tylenol. It got worse, so I took another, and then another. I was shivering and thirsty, irritated and hot. My teeth itched and my hair hurt. *Maybe it's a bug*, I thought, running to my tiny Chinatown bathroom to evacuate, simultaneously, the contents of my stomach and bowels, grateful, as I had never been, for the compact space and proximity of the sink to the pot. A piercing center point of pain on the right side of my head haloed out in dull waves. Thoughts crashed together hard and loud. Bright and nonsensical. Glaring cartoonish nightmares. Would it help if I drilled a hole in my skull or bashed it in with a hammer? After three days, the only solution, it seemed, was to throw myself out the window.

Instead, I managed to take a cab to St. Vincent's Hospital in the West Village. I ran in screaming, *Help me! Help me!* They saw me right away. Stroke? Meningitis? I woke up hours later in a darkened room with a sheet over my head. There were IVs with fluids and pain medication. There was a heaviness in my body and mind, but the pain was gone, and I could have cried with relief. The nurse asked me, why, besides the fact that I was Irish, had it taken me so long to come in? She was Irish-American with an Irish name on her nametag. What was it? Sadhbh? Níamh? Aoife? I tried to explain that the synapses required to put on my shoes, grab my wallet and keys, go outside and hail a cab were just not firing. It took me so long to come in because I had lost the capacity to function. I managed to say the words:

"I couldn't figure out my shoes."

She nodded. "Sounds like a migraine," she said. "You'll have to follow up with your GP."

Migraine? *A headache?*

As I was leaving, she called after me, "You know, the ancient Celts believed the skull was the seat of the soul."

I followed up with my doctor to find out what I had to do to ensure I never experienced one of those "headaches" again. If it was, in fact, a migraine, he said, most likely there would be more, periodically, episodically or chronically. It's a complicated disease. No two migraineurs are the same. He said there is something of a spectrum, and we would have to figure out what my triggers were. He handed me a chart, a faded photocopy on which I would track for three months how I ate, drank, thought, slept, menstruated, and felt. He sent me away with some sumatriptan pills and the instruction to take one "as soon as the migraine approaches, or better yet, *before* the migraine approaches."

I lived in terror of another migraine approaching. Another one did, a month after the first. Over the next few months, a pattern emerged. I got a migraine right before my period. For some, migraine can be triggered by lights, sounds, smells, alcohol, certain foods, skipping meals, not getting enough sleep, getting too much sleep, stress, emotional strain, physical exertion, exercise for example, even orgasm. My trigger turned out to be hormonal: the fluctuations of estrogen during my cycle wreak havoc inside me. The endocrine system, the body's messaging service, erroneously pings the vascular and sends blood rushing and swelling through the intricate structure of arteries, veins and capillaries threaded through my brain.

I began to recognize the phases: the *prodrome* brought irritability, anxiety, and racing thoughts. The *aura* brought sensory disturbances; some people see lights or shapes, I smell electrical wires burning and have heightened sensitivity to light, colors, sounds, smells. The *headache phase* brought nausea, shivering, and intense head pain. Finally, the *postdrome phase* brought a short burst of wellbeing followed by exhaustion. Coupled with pre-menstrual tension and period cramps, these episodes lasted about five days. While the pills helped with head pain, the other symptoms persisted, and I had to spend two days a month in bed, then three, then four.

The truth is, very little is known about this neuro-logical condition and its physiological behaviors, despite the fact that it has been accounted for by physicians, healers, mystics, and poets from all over the world for thousands of years. The earliest account can be found in ancient Egypt around 1200 BCE, and specific symptoms were recorded by Hippocrates, Aretaeus of Cappadocia, and the Persian physician Abu Bakr Muhammad ibn Zakariyya al-Razi. The word "migraine" was first used by the second-century physician Galenus of Pergamon. It derives from the Latin *hemicrania*, *hemi* being "half" and *crania* being "skull."

The Chinese surgeon Huà Tuó, during the late Han Dynasty, used acupuncture to relieve migraine symptoms. In the Middle Ages, the German abbess and Christian mystic Hildegard of Bingen used herbal medicine to treat her illness. She deduced that God would only inflict one side of her head at a time, because if he inflicted both sides, the pain would be unendurable. Some have suggested that migraine's aura may have influenced her ecstatic writing:

And I saw as if in the middle of the southern sky an image, beautiful and wonderful in the mystery of God, like a human in form. Her face was of such beauty and radiance that I could more easily look at the sun than her.

A popular treatment at this time was trepanning, the boring of a hole through the skull. Trepanning was a practice used to treat a variety of injuries and illnesses, and trepanned skulls have been found all over the world as far back as far as the Neolithic period. Though it is said that these holes were made to release evil, pain-causing spirits, I am sure it was an ancestor in the throes of the headache phase who came up with this particular solution.

In her essay *On Being Ill*, Virginia Woolf asks why, given the nature and ubiquity of illness, it has not taken its place alongside love, battle, and jealousy as one of the great themes of literature. There is ample language to describe love, she says, but a sufferer has none to describe a headache to a doctor. This may be, she suggests, because literature has primarily concerned itself with productions of the mind, whereas illness is also a concern of the body. She says new language would have to be invented by taking "pain in one hand, and a lump of pure sound in the other (as perhaps the people of Babel did in the beginning), so to crush them together that a brand-new word in the end drops out."

For Woolf, there is something partly mystical about illness. She says there is much to be learned in the "undiscovered countries" occupied by those confined to bed. Woolf's preoccupation with time is sketched out here. She makes the association between clock-time and "the armies of the upright" who march on into the future. In illness, we lay prone. No longer accountable to the strictness of marching time, we encounter the opportunity to look at the world in new ways. In this space, there are other rules at play, less conformity, and a different sense of time, and here, instead of fighting to remain upright, we might surrender and allow the mysteries that lie beneath the mundanities of our lives to surface and reveal themselves.

In 1931, a wealthy American businessman, Roland Hazzard, having sought every possible treatment for alcoholism in the US, consulted Jung in Switzerland. Jung told Hazzard he was a hopeless case and only a deep and affecting spiritual conversion would save him. The young man returned to the US and joined the Oxford Group, a religious organization based on first-century Christianity. The members were mostly upper- and middle-class white men, and many found help for their alcoholism here. The community stressed surrender to God, self-examination, public confession, restitution and helping others. As part of this program, Hazzard tried to help his alcoholic friend, Ebby Thacher. Thacher, in turn, tried to help his alcoholic friend, Bill Wilson.

During Wilson's final hospitalization for alcoholism, he complained to the physician that, in order to stay sober, he had to help other alcoholics and he had been unable to. The doctor suggested that, rather than preaching all the God stuff, he might just share his own drinking story. His pain, his experience. His words. Wilson took the doctor's advice when he reached out to Bob Smith, a doctor with advanced alcoholism living in Akron, Ohio.

In 1935, these two men co-founded Alcoholics Anonymous. All over the world, twelve-step programs have grown out of this moment. One sick person, as they say, relating to another the true nature of their malady. Humans with life-destroying addictions to alcohol, drugs, food, shopping, gambling, sex, etc., find entry to recovery in the mirroring of their own experience in another person's. The particulars of individual lives may vary vastly, but through identification with thoughts, feelings, and emotions, vital connections are made. A new language had entered the collective consciousness. Bill Wilson published the *Big Book of Alcoholics Anonymous* in 1939, and the language found in it continues to spread around the world. It may not have been intended as a literary work, but it was written with a literary sensibility. It is the story of transformation for its authors and its readers. And today, the *Big Book of Alcoholics Anonymous* remains, for better or worse, one of the bestselling books of all time.

On Being Ill was written in the mid-1920s, a decade before these strides in the fields of psychoanalysis and twelve-step recovery. Perhaps Woolf, given the time she spent in the undiscovered countries of illness, was well placed to anticipate these developments.

She ends her essay by relating a book she read while she was sick. It is not a great work of literature, she tells us, but her mind, altered by illness, found pleasure in it. It is the tale of an aristocratic English household going to rack and ruin in the mid-nineteenth century. There are two daughters who, Woolf points out, are hardly individual entities, coming as they do from the all-consuming web of old English family connections. They are not made to come into the full expression of their humanity. In Jungian terms they are unindividuated selves. "Charlotte and Louisa grew up in their incomparable loveliness, with pencils in their hands, forever sketching, dancing, flirting, in a cloud of gauze."

Both girls are married off to husbands in the colonies, Charlotte in India and Louisa "dumped down in Ireland with Lord Waterford." Lord Waterford spends his days hunting and lonely Louisa spends hers sketching and doing good works in the community: visiting the sick, putting on plays with local children, and making murals for the church. There is, of course, a famine simmering in the background. A mass annihilation that barely touches her life. When her husband dies in a hunting accident, we are given a glimpse of Louisa's powerlessness, rage, and pain. She cannot articulate it, but on the morning of the funeral, we see "the curtain, heavy, mid-Victorian, plush perhaps, was all crushed together where she had grasped it in her agony." I confess, unlike generations of students and Woolf scholars, it is not with poor Louisa and her inability to express herself that my sympathies lie.

I ask my American university classmates to consider the words "dumped down in Ireland." They blink blankly, the phrase does not sting them the way it does me. They do not know the colonial history of England in Ireland, and why would they? The English themselves, even today, do not know it. If England were to look honestly at its history in Ireland, it would have to look honestly at its history in India and Australia and Africa and Asia and parts of North and South America, and what nation would want to face all that? I recognize in England's leadership a kind of bottoming-out, like a drunk in their last days of drinking, pushing everyone away who might help them, becoming more and more isolated, desperately holding on to an old idea of themselves. Espousing grandiosities even as everyone can see they have soiled themselves.

We might extend a hand to say, when you are ready, we can talk, but our ancestors are here now, and we have to tend to them. Our healing does not depend on you facing yourself, but yours does.

In the last few years, migraine communities have flourished online. They examine the pros and cons of new treatments: Botox, Aimovig, Starve and Sink. They discuss the intersections of other illnesses; they share hardships and offer support and encouragement. In 2018, when a social media influencer posted a picture doing the "migraine pose," placing a hand on their head as if they had a headache, members of the migraine community responded by flooding the internet with images of themselves at home, sick in bed doing the real "migraine pose": faces with swelling on one side, flushed and dry complexions, sallow, pain-dazed eyes; I recognized them all, as reflections in a thousand fragmented mirrors.

Actions like this let us know we are not alone. Through these communities, I learned the term for when your hair hurts: allodynia; and the one for when your speech is jumbled: transient aphasia. I had no language for these symptoms, but naming them has given me the power to trust the experience of my body, and to dismiss claims that the pain "is all in your head." I have learned that migraine is physical but, like all illness, it can affect us mentally, emotionally, and spiritually.

There is a saying in recovery, *Time Takes Time*. It takes time for some root causes and conditions to push up through our consciousness. *Time Takes Time*. It is also a reminder to keep our focus in the moment, not to be racing off into the future and forgetting where we are, so the years don't rush on lived only in our heads and not in our bodies. Migraine taught Joan Didion this lesson, what she calls the "imposed yoga of concentrating on the pain." Of not fighting it, of being with it. She moves through the cycle to the other side with a renewed sense of aliveness and gratitude.

In ancient Ireland, the final harvest feast of Samhain— now celebrated October 31 to November 1—signified the end of one cycle and the beginning of the next. It is also Celtic New Year and, just as the Celtic day begins at dusk, so the new year begins going into the darkest months. The Celts valued and respected the dark, and knew it was as necessary as light for unity and wholeness. At this feast, the veil that separates this corporeal world from the world of divinities, spirits, and the dead was at its thinnest and most porous. Unlike the structure of Christian otherworlds, the Otherworld of the Celts exists beside our own. Not above or below. Time moves so slowly in that world that an hour spent there would correspond to a century here. At Samhain, beings from that world can cross easily into ours and we into theirs. Crossings can also happen at the thin places that are dotted all over the Celtic lands of Ireland, Scotland, Brittany, Cornwall, Dover: special places by a holy well, or under a certain oak tree, where the worlds are always very close together. Illness, I believe, can also bring us to the thin places where the borders between the spiritual, physical, mental, and emotional temporarily dissolve.

I woke with thoughts racing and had the feeling they had been racing through my dreams. I forced myself out of bed and fought through waves of darkness and desolation to brush the teeth. Feed the dog. Make the tea. Planting one foot in front of the other, I walked to the train, wondering how I would make it through this day. The announcements at the station were abusively loud, though no one else seemed to notice. I found a seat on the train and sat gratefully. I smelled electric wires burning and looked around for the source before realizing it was inside my head. The headache would follow, so I rooted through my bag for the medication. The train moved and I was overwhelmed by other scents: fresh sweat beneath a powdery perfume from a woman at the other end of the car; a packed lunch of leftovers in the backpack of the man next to me. I could hear the tinny *tze-tze-tze* from the earphones of a teenaged boy, and over this I could hear every syllable of every word spoken in every conversation. I watched the thoughts of the other passengers as they rushed into my mind and I could see, suddenly, how all the disparate fragments of an essay I was working on might come together. I swallowed the pill without water. The cells of my body opened and fused with the plastic seat, as the steel from the track traveled up the length of my spine. There was a roll of nausea, a crack of perspiration. And I knew, just for a moment, that there is no separation between me and you, and all who have gone before. That all is interconnected and interdependent. I knew too that this is what the mystics, down the ages, have been telling us, but from the brighter side, the light side of their heads.

Part Four
Samhain

November
Harvest

After I put the drink down, the long process of healing began. Slowly, I withdrew from activities that no longer fed me. I no longer kept company that drained me. I left the theatre if a performance bored me. I closed a book if it did not hold my interest. Time became my most treasured resource, and I guarded it protectively. I wrote and wrote with an urgency that quickened between the #MeToo exposures in the fall of 2017 and the abortion referendum in Ireland in May of 2018.

For years prior, I had been writing late into the night, letting the dishes pile up. Every article I read, every film I saw, every conversation I had yielded fruit for my work. The world shimmered and pinged with connections. And after half a decade of living in this ecstasy, I ended up with a large unwieldy manuscript that nobody wanted to read.

But I knew this book was in there, so I enrolled in an interdisciplinary master's program at the CUNY

Graduate Center to help me find it. In one of my first courses, the professor, who had done her graduate work at Queen's University, Belfast, asked if I had ever heard of the Irish women who were used for gynecological experiments in New York hospitals in the mid-nineteenth century. I had not.

Mary Smith was a young woman, and a sick and destitute mother when she arrived in New York in the early 1850s, shortly after the Great Famine. She came from the west of Ireland, the area most impacted by the disaster. In 1855, she was admitted to the newly opened Woman's Hospital on 28th and Madison. According to its founder and chief surgeon, J. Marion Sims, the hospital was the first of its kind devoted solely to the diseases of women, and Mary Smith is listed in their records as the first surgical patient. While examining her, Sims found the worst case of obstetric fistula he had ever seen. Vesicovaginal fistula, an injury sustained during childbirth or sexual violence, is a perforation between the wall of the vagina and the bladder, causing constant incontinence and considerable discomfort. Sims located a hard, greyish mass protruding through

Smith's fistula. It was embedded in scar tissue, crusted over and saturated with urine. Before she had left Ireland, a physician had inserted a wooden ball from a fishing net to prevent her bladder from collapsing. Over the next seven years, without anesthesia, and in front of mostly male audiences, Sims performed more than thirty experimental surgeries on Mary Smith.

On April 17, 2018, the City of New York removed a statue of J. Marion Sims from its pedestal on Fifth Avenue and 103rd Street. This East Harlem neighborhood is up the road from where I worked for many years as a personal assistant. My office was located in a grand Madison Avenue apartment building with warrens of "maid's rooms" on the lower floors. Today, these rooms are used for storage: Christmas decorations and golf clubs, bicycles and winter boots. In small spaces like these, Irish immigrant women of the past lived close at hand, at the beck and call of the families in their luxurious quarters on the floors above. Occasionally, I took the elevator down to visit, opening the doors quickly, in the hope of catching a glimpse of their shapes pressed into the dusty afternoon air, before they had time to disappear, fully, back into their ghost worlds.

In East Harlem the streets segregate neighbors along social, economic, and racial lines. Following the 2006 publication of Harriet A. Washington's *Medical Apartheid: The Dark History of Medical Experimentation on Black Americans from Colonial Times to the Present*, resident and activist groups began calling for the removal of the Sims statue, insisting its presence, and the history it represented, was offensive to the Black and Latina women of the neighborhood. After the lethal Unite the Right rally in Charlottesville, Virginia, in 2017, which was organized in response to the proposed removal of a statue of Confederate general Robert E. Lee, local activists increased their efforts. They spoke about the resonance of the past in the present and the intergenerational traumas suffered in their families and communities.

Sims had been a plantation doctor in Alabama in the 1840s and early 1850s. In a deal struck with local plantation owners, he set up a hut where he could treat enslaved women afflicted with various gynecological ailments, including vesicovaginal fistula. The women lived in the hut, and here, Sims performed life-threatening, experimental surgeries without anesthesia. The women did chores in exchange for treatment while Sims honed his craft, including his groundbreaking surgery to cure vesicovaginal fistula. When he succeeded, the women went back to work on the plantations, and Sims took his new skills to New York City.

With the support of a group of prominent women, Sims opened the Woman's Hospital, a charitable institution where he could demonstrate his procedures. The board of "Lady Managers" required that Sims employ a woman doctor to be his surgical assistant. Sims agreed, but on meeting Thomas Addis Emmet, a fellow Southerner, Sims insisted the young Irish-American doctor be hired instead.

My professor recommended that I read *Medical Bondage: Race, Gender, and the Origins of American Gynecology* by Dr. Deirdre Cooper Owens. I learned that in the free North, Sims did not have access to enslaved women's bodies as he did in the South, but another population presented itself: poor Irish immigrant women, many of whom were famine refugees. According to Cooper Owens, the prevailing attitudes toward the bodies of these women were that they were "not quite white" and, like African-American women, they were considered hyper-sexual, excessively fertile, made of tougher stuff, and capable of enduring more physical pain than white women. Anesthesia was coming into use in the 1850s, but racist attitudes persisted and it was not until 1865 that the Woman's Hospital began to use it, and even then, only in "special cases."

Both Emmet and Sims wrote autobiographies, so they had the opportunity to fashion the narratives of their lives. For posterity, they outlined their personal and professional achievements. Mary Smith appears in a pamphlet of a talk given by Emmet in 1893 to the Alumni Association of the Woman's Hospital. He describes the ailing woman as "a most offensive and loathsome object," and goes on to discuss the removal of the wooden ball from her body. First, he praises Sims: "After a remarkable display of patience and dexterity, Dr. Sims finally succeeded in removing it." Touching on the patient's experience: "It was done, however, amid her screams and intense suffering."

There was professional jealousy between Emmet and Sims. Emmet claims that it was he, and not Sims, who cured Mary Smith. He performed many of her thirty-four surgeries, even fashioning a new urethra among other successful outcomes; however, when she began to suffer discomfort, Emmet blamed her, saying the trouble was "brought on by her constant imprudence."

Smith approached Sims for help, and against Emmet's wishes, Sims performed an operation to remove a bladder stone. In doing so, he undid the delicate work Emmet had done. Mary Smith had been living at the hospital, doing chores in exchange for treatment, but when her body could withstand no more surgeries, she was turned out on the street. She hung around the hospital, "a common street beggar," until she was hit by carriage and killed a couple of years later.

The Woman's Hospital records are now located at the Arthur H. Aufses, Jr., MD Archives at the Icahn School of Medicine at Mount Sinai, across from the empty pedestal on which the statue of J. Marion Sims used to stand. As part of my graduate work, I made an appointment to see the archives. The patient casebooks list column after column of Irish names: Callaghans, Connells, Egans, O'Briens. There are a number of Mary Smiths. Most of the women had been born in Ireland, married in their teens and given birth seven, eight, thirteen times. Though we cannot know their individual stories, a sad narrative emerges: societal norms of racism, sexism, and classism enabled the medical establishment to perform experiments on the bodies of marginalized women for the ultimate benefit of more privileged communities. Mary Smith was not an anomaly, and for Deirdre Cooper Owens she has "come to represent the thousands of poor, Irish immigrant women who were connected to New York City's hospitals."

Taking a break in the Starbucks on the ground floor, I sat among hospital researchers and interns, staring out at the pouring rain, anger and sadness burning in my chest. Maybe it's too much, I thought, ingesting all this history. Perhaps I should change tack. Avert my gaze. Pour my energies into something lighter. I watched the smokers huddle beneath the awning and wished I still smoked, so I could distract myself for a minute, by going out to join them.

When Irish people hear the name Thomas Addis Emmet they might think of the elder Thomas of the heroic Emmet family. They might know that he and his brother, Robert, were members of the United Irishmen, a radical political group inspired by the ideals of the American Revolution, who fought for an end to British monarchical rule in Ireland. They might know that following the failed rebellion of 1803, Robert was executed by the British, and that today, multiple memorials commemorate his name, including the recently dedicated Robert Emmet Park in Washington, DC. They might also know that his brother Thomas emigrated to the United States, where he was a passionate abolitionist who went on to become the New York State Attorney General. An obelisk commemorates his life in the graveyard of St. Paul's Chapel at the foot of the World Trade Center. They are less likely to know that Thomas's son, John Patten Emmet, became a slaveholder and professor—with a resonant connection to the present—at the University of Virginia at Charlottesville. The invitation to his post came from Thomas Jefferson himself. John's son, Thomas, named for his grandfather, went on to become the doctor associated with J. Marion Sims, one of the most controversial figures in modern medicine. Given their connection, it is surprising that the younger Thomas's reputation has never come into question.

In my final year of graduate school, I went looking for Dr. Thomas Addis Emmet in Ireland. It was a grey day, windy and wet, when my dad dropped me off at Ireland's national cemetery in Dublin. Coming from Ashbourne, I used to pass the high stone walls of Glasnevin Cemetery every day on my way to school and work, but I was detached from Ireland's history back then; it was heavy

and impenetrable, a darkness in the consciousness, not buried exactly, but not exactly accessible.

In recent years, Glasnevin Cemetery has become a popular destination for tourists, and as a long-term emigrant, I had become something of a tourist on my home turf. At the information desk, I inquired about the location of the Emmet memorial. A young man pointed into the near distance. "See that huge Celtic cross?" he asked. I could hardly miss it, standing erect against the low sky, in pride of place just inside the gates.

Sims is still commemorated around the world. There are even IVF treatment clinics named for him in Ireland. Emmet also made the history books for his contributions to the fields of gynecology and plastic surgery. Wanting to align himself with his heroic forebears, Emmet requested that upon his death, both his remains and those of his Irish-patriot grandfather be brought to Glasnevin Cemetery, and laid to rest in the same country as Robert, their martyred relative. The imposing memorial cross was carved by James and Willie Pearce, father and brother of Patrick Pearce, the revolutionary hero of the 1916 Rising, another failed Irish rebellion, but one that led, after an arduous struggle against British rule, to Ireland's independence in 1922. As I read the bombastic dedication, a smaller Celtic cross, just yards away, caught my eye. I walked over and read the inscription. In 2016, the president of Ireland, Michael D. Higgins, dedicated this memorial to the victims of *an Gorta Mór*. In the short distance between these two symbols lie the stories of Mary Smith and the Irish emigrant women whose bodies were used and abused by the medical establishment in New York's hospitals.

The question haunts me: as an Irish woman who emigrated to New York in the last links of the unbroken

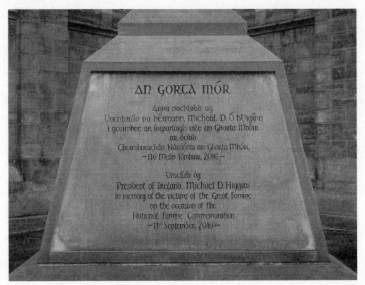

chain of mass emigration since the Famine, why had I never heard of these women in the first links? There is a connection between us and between all women, and all people in the margins of patriarchal societies, in the historic struggle for bodily autonomy.

I walked under my umbrella through the cemetery, and recognized the graves of many notable characters from Ireland's turbulent history. The old stones, the grand trees, the magpies and the crows. This graveyard opened in 1832, and it was designed to be a place of "memorial and contemplation." I thought about who gets remembered and who gets forgotten, and how and why, about all the rhetoric that surrounds heroic monuments. I wondered if there had been reluctance to acknowledge Thomas Addis Emmet's relationship to J. Marion Sims because of the Emmet family's sacrosanct name in Irish and Irish-American politics. To acknowledge the relationship would involve casting a cold eye over the entanglement of Irish roots in American racism and, in this case, their uncomfortable proximity to the anti-colonial roots of Irish national-ism. But in order to talk about the lives of ordinary women like Mary Smith, we have to start somewhere. I circled back to the Famine cross, and invited the story

if it wanted to be told through me. Then, walking on,
I turned my back to the Emmet memorial, and exited
the gate to wait in the rain for the next bus home.

December
The Longest Night

People who have recently lost someone have a certain look, recognizable maybe only to those who have seen that look on their own faces. I have noticed it on my face and I notice it now on others. The look is one of extreme vulnerability, nakedness, openness. It is the look of someone who walks from the ophthalmologist's office into the bright daylight with dilated eyes, or of someone who wears glasses and is suddenly made to take them off. These people who have lost someone look naked because they think themselves invisible. I myself felt invisible for a period of time, incorporeal.

—Joan Didion, *The Year of Magical Thinking*

I was, for a time, taken aback by my reflection in shop windows, by the fleeting glimpses of it in passing subway cars, by the face in the mirror, before I fully inhabited it. I was jarred by seeing the kind of transparency I recognized from times of grief, because no one had died. I saw it too in the faces of my parents and my brothers and sisters. It settled in photos and flickered across the screen during FaceTime and WhatsApp video calls. From 2016–2021, my brother, let's call him Ben, had been in a high-security psychiatric hospital in Dublin. A year passed, then two. The grief rose, but it did not release. How to put into words the fact that he was there, but he was lost to us? And how suddenly it hit home that he was never coming back.

Joan Didion says we tell ourselves stories in order to live. Our stories tend to follow an established plot structure. They arise in the temporal and progress in a linear way: they have a beginning, middle, and end. But what of stories that arise and do not progress and do not end? How do we tell these stories, so we too might live?

In December 2016, Ben walked into my parent's kitchen, took a knife from the drawer, went into the front room where my elderly father was watching television and, in a frenzied attack, stabbed him multiple times from behind. Ben threw my mother to the ground and left my father for dead with the blade still in his back. He then wandered down to the village, and in The Stags Head, he ordered a pint, sat down with blood-stained hands, and drank it.

My sister Maria called me at my office in New York. She was crying and could barely get the words out. She did not know at that point if our father was going to make it. I screamed loudly before my voice contracted into the back of my throat. Of the three hundred contacts in my phone, not one felt safe. I could not imagine forming the words, speaking them, or having them be received. So I finished my work day, took the subway home, walked the dog, ordered a pizza, and watched Netflix.

My father spent the night in the ICU propped up on his side until a specialist surgeon could be brought in the following day to remove the knife. When they arrived at the hospital, a nurse told my sister it wasn't the only stabbing that night. It was always hectic, she said, on the night of a full moon. We were, just then, days away from the winter solstice, the longest night of the year, a celestial event that has been celebrated for millennia at Newgrange in County Meath, only a short drive from my family's home.

My father survived, but my sisters said that whenever they left their houses, they felt as if everyone was looking at them and talking about what had happened. I was unable to leave my apartment for a few days, and in the weeks after, I did so only when absolutely necessary. The world felt sharp and hostile, so even the smallest errand became a huge undertaking.

There are nine children in my family. Growing up, Ben always had a lot to say for himself. If there was anything of note about him, it was that he had, unlike the rest of us, a huge and varied vocabulary. He loved to hear himself yammering on about Cú Chulainn, archeology, Egypt, the "Magic Mandrake", "Bohemian Rhapsody". The rest of us had no interest in his constant stream of observations and opinions. His voice just grated on our nerves, and we would tell him to shut up. We were always telling each other to shut up. Shut up, you! *You*, shut up!

Ben grew tall and good-looking. He went out with a beautiful girl and he had many good friends. He was a gifted athlete, a long-distance runner, and in his early teens was even training for the Olympic team. When Peter died, Ben turned to alcohol and drugs. We all did. In Ireland in 1998, grief counseling was not a thing. Drugs were. Drink was. So, we all suffered in our own ways, alone, together.

Like Peter, Ben took up guitar, and he surprised us with his talent. He covered Coldplay and Radiohead tunes—acoustic versions—before writing his own songs. The lyrics were often poetic and complicated. Like many young Irish people, he saved a small sum and went backpacking around Europe with his friends. They stopped and worked when they needed to. They planted and picked, made more friends, played guitar, sang songs, drank beer, and smoked hash. Inevitably, my parents would get a call. They would roll their eyes and bail him out of whatever fix he had got himself into: the season ended, the money ran out, the wallet got stolen, the passport lost.

For a while, Ben settled in Dublin, and he and his friends shared a big house in Ranelagh. He got a job in the coffee shop across the street. He was the tall, skinny lad with the long, tangled hair and dilated pupils, who stood out front smoking cigarettes, always happy to natter with the customers. He was easygoing and kind, so people probably overlooked the filthy fingernails that cupped their coffees as he handed them over the counter.

On St. Patrick's Day 2012, Ben was out in Dublin, celebrating with friends. At some point in the night, he disappeared. A week later, his friends found him in his room, terrified by something that had happened that night. The story changed every time he told it. He was pursued, he was injected, he was raped. My brothers Martin and John convinced him to go to the hospital to get checked out. The doctor said he needed help, but he would have to stop drinking and drugging first. He moved back in with my parents who began a campaign of care which included indulging his desire for certain foods, bargaining with him to take a shower, walking him around the house to assure him all the windows and doors were locked, and engaging in his complex arguments about the time-traveling abilities of the psychopaths who were pursuing him from other dimensions.

Ben became obsessed with the National Lottery. He knew he was going to win. Every week, my family, not wanting to take any chances, gave him their euros and played his winning numbers. Every week, to his utter disbelief, he lost. One night, my mother Skyped me. Ben was agitated and insisted on seeing my new apartment. I twirled my laptop around, enabling a full view of my three-hundred-square-foot Manhattan studio. He side-eyed me suspiciously. He was just curious, he said, to see what I had bought with the Lotto money. There was no convincing him that the studio was a rental, or that it was tiny, or that I had not won the Lotto, nor had I, in fact, stolen the winning numbers from his mind.

When I visited, I found my family home on edge. My sisters refused to bring their children around because Ben frightened them. Bone-thin and jumpy, he spent hours in front of the television, half watching *Friends* re-runs, drinking tea, and smoking cigarettes, and half staring into space and laughing to himself.

With each new doctor, or treatment plan, or medication, Ben might improve for a few weeks, but then he would regress, always a little bit further than before. As the illness progressed, we were all drawn into its supernatural world. He saw and heard things and predicted outlandish episodes that came to pass: "Look at the scar," he instructed us, pointing to nothing on his head, "it's from when they operated on me in India and took a piece of my brain." His behaviors became increasingly bizarre. He wrote "the greatest song ever written," then took a bus to a recording studio in Dublin and demanded they record it. When they asked him to leave, he accused them of stealing his music. Characters and scenes from movies overlapped seamlessly with his life. He would spin tales about our father or one of his friends, or some random neighbor who happened to pass the house. One by one, we were all made part of the conspiracy against him. He was stressed and panicked all the time. There were psychopaths everywhere. They followed him into his dreams, so even in sleep he had no peace.

Ben lost a lot of weight and his face darkened and sank. His suffering was unendurable. And it was unendurable for us to witness someone we loved in so much fear and pain without being able to provide any comfort. At first, he beseeched us with agonized eyes. We went from trying to convince him there was nothing there to trying to convince him we would do anything to protect him. Why had we not called the police? he wanted to know. Why are we all acting like everything was normal? He turned away from us little by little and did not turn back.

He ended up in the hospital, where he was finally diagnosed with paranoid schizophrenia. Often this diagnosis is met with terror, but we were relieved. It meant Ben could finally get treatment tailored to his needs. The doctors told my parents that the problem was not Ben's schizophrenia as such, it was the fact that he had no insight. Patients with insight can suffer the same symptoms as those without, but they understand, to varying degrees, that what is happening to them is part of their illness, not shared reality. With treatment, they can often recover their lives. But without insight, the doctors said, there really wasn't much hope.

Things would go well for a while until they wouldn't. The delusions and hallucinations. The constant swing from hope to no hope. My siblings and I talked incessantly, and Ben was all we talked about. What was to be done? A long-term care facility? A home? Our parents could no longer cope, but they would not hear of it. They downplayed his episodes and hovered protectively over him, they would take his suffering on themselves because they would not have him taken from them, because they could not bear to lose another child.

Ben was hospitalized multiple times, but he always managed to escape. The police chased him all over our housing estate. Our mother told us not to be discussing his business with the neighbors. We told her, *They have eyes!* She brought her own stuff to the situation. We all did. Finally, Ben agreed to an outpatient treatment program. Every day, a nurse came to our house to administer his medication, and every other day, he saw his counselor in a clinic in the village. He hated the way the medications made him feel. It was a gross injustice, he said, being forced to take medication when there was nothing wrong with you.

One day he came home and said his counselor was taking his group on a weekend trip to Galway. My parents were delighted. A bit of socializing would do him good. My mother helped him pack a bag. Underwear, deodorant, socks. He slung his guitar over his shoulder, waved goodbye, and off he went. On Monday, my brother Martin got an email: "I'm in India. I'm fine. Don't look for me." He had booked himself a one-way ticket, got on a plane, and left.

We did not know how much money he had, but we knew that he had no medication and that he was alone. Our local police contacted Interpol, who said they would only be able to locate him when his name showed up in the system. The world suddenly became vast and unknowable. Our little brother was very ill, and he was out there in it. We lived in fight or flight mode: jumping on ringing phones, checking email a hundred times a day. Constantly texting: *Any news?* Things that mattered before mattered less. Our lives stalled, all our energies focused on the single point of Ben.

My family forwarded each other countless articles from our hours of Google research. There were pieces about the late onset of schizophrenia, the correlation between marijuana, schizophrenia, and violence, capitalism and schizophrenia. I found a talk by Gabor Maté about how Western culture is making people sick. According to him, the best place for a person with schizophrenia is in a village in India. I quickly sent it to my family, maybe Ben was guided there? I said. Maybe he is a shaman or a druid? Who is to say these medications are the answer? Sitting around in dull hospital rooms drugged up to the eyeballs. Maybe we should trust the universe to take care of him. Maybe on some deep level, he knows what is best for himself?

The call came from the Irish Embassy. There was a nun from the Missionaries of Charity in Kolkata, Mother Teresa's convent, with a message for Ben's parents. She wanted to let them know that he was in a very bad way. He was emaciated and living on the streets. He had no shoes. She fed him biscuits every day. They talked. In all likelihood, she said, spirits had entered him. He was hanging around the temples. She had seen it before. Evil spirits.

My mother called me. "Do you think?"

"She is supposed to be a Catholic!" I shrieked, trying to keep everything in its box.

"But didn't Jesus cast out spirits out of people?"

"The people probably had schizophrenia!" I yelled, to dispel both our fears that Ben had been possessed by evil spirits. I spent the rest of the evening googling all incidences of demon possession in the Bible. When the nun told Ben that his family were on their way, he upped and disappeared again.

The next call came from Interpol. Ben had shown up in a hospital in Mumbai. He was recovering from brain surgery. We were unhinged with disbelief. All the times we searched through his hair for the invisible scar he insisted was there. He had been busking for money when a man tried to take his guitar. Ben hit the guy, and the guy's three sons came back and beat Ben brutally. The hospital said come and get him out of here, or he will end up in jail, or dead on the street.

Martin and John made the trip to bring him home. Ben, even in his weakened state, found the energy to tell them to get out. They begged and pleaded. He told them to fuck off. They told him he was loved and that was all they could do.

The next call: he had been arrested in Delhi. The details were confused. He was swimming near a sacred site. He was walking near a military site. He had a beard and a backpack. Acting very suspicious. Was he a terrorist? They would need five hundred euros to process his case. My parents wired the money immediately. The case was not as simple as it seemed, there would be another hearing, another seven hundred, he would need a lawyer, another thousand euros. We marked our calendars and counted down the days to each new hearing. Each time, a larger sum was needed, fourteen hundred euros. Two thousand euros.

In addition to funneling money, my parent's full-time jobs became daily rounds of calls and emails to the Department of Foreign Affairs, the Health and Safety Executive, Ben's doctors, the Irish Embassy, every local politician, the lawyers in India, and the Irish Minister for Health. Ben was caught up in a Kafkaesque nightmare of bureaucracy, the frayed remnants of British colonial rule. He had not actually been charged with anything, but the months passed and his passport expired, and that was a whole other problem. The lawyers told my parents that Ben was a polite and well-behaved young man, and when he got out of jail in India, he wished to go to Thailand. My parents tried to convince them that Ben was very ill, that he needed urgent medical attention, and that yes, he did train for the Irish Olympic team, but no, they did not steal his Lotto money. Almost a year later, when it was becoming clear that Ben wasn't going anywhere, they apologized to my parents for not believing them. Ben had been sent to solitary confinement. There was a violent episode, they said, when he was served a boiled egg for breakfast. The shell, apparently, had a crack in it.

Irish politicians came to our house. My mother made them pots of tea while my father explained the situation. He showed them the doctors' and hospital letters. They expressed outrage that this could be happening to an Irish citizen. They shook my parents' hands as they left and promised to do everything in their power to bring Ben home. The days passed, the weeks, my parents called their offices, were put on hold, their assistants took messages.

* * *

Nothing happens in isolation. My alcoholism doesn't just happen to me, as much as I wish it did. It affects every relationship in my life, whether I am drinking or not. The tightness in the belly, the stone in the shoe, the constant itch to be anywhere but here. This is my default setting, and if untreated, it seeps out and sours the air wherever I go. Ben's illness affects all of us too. We are connected in ways we do not even understand. In her diary dated 1 July 1903, Virginia Woolf wrote:

> I think I see for a moment how our minds are all threaded together—how any live mind today is of the very same stuff as Plato's & Euripides. It is only a continuation & development of the same thing. It is this common mind that binds the whole world together; & all the world is mind.

After almost two years in India, most of it spent in prison, all of it without medication, the Irish government finally arranged for a trained escort to bring Ben home. An ambulance picked him up from Dublin Airport and drove him to the hospital, where he was given a physical exam. He was then sent to wait for the staff psychiatrist, who was to see him later that day. Ben simply stood up, got dressed, and walked out, unnoticed. In the pouring Irish rain, he hailed a cab to my parents' house.

My parents had been over at the Blanchardstown Shopping Center. My father needed a new jacket. They ran the errand, expecting to hear word from the hospital later that evening, but when they turned the corner onto their street, they saw the taxi, and Ben standing at the front door, his T-shirt and sweatpants soaked through, his rattan flip-flops disintegrating. Thin and shaking and totally vulnerable. There was no way they would be sending him back to the hospital. They ran to him and threw their arms around him. He told them to pay the taxi.

Nothing my siblings and I said could make my parents send their son back to the hospital. We begged and pleaded and tried to understand. I asked my siblings, if it were their son, would they do different? They exhaled, all the fire gone from their fight. The police came and my parents signed a form. Ben was their ward now. Did they understand that he would actually have to *do* something before the police could intervene? Did they understand?

Two months later, Ben stabbed our father. He claimed it was self-defense. There would be a trial. Our father, still in bandages, went to the police station to make his statement. While Ben was in prison, we got word that he was to be moved to Dublin's Central Mental Hospital. In a 2018 interview with the *Irish Times*, the director of the hospital, Professor Harry Kennedy, said: "The most typical patient is a man suffering from schizophrenia who has stopped taking his medication and has killed a family member—often a parent." Professor Kennedy told my parents that there are many young men with Ben's illness untreated in the prison system, and many, many more on the streets. Whenever I pass that person in the subway or in the public restroom, I think of all the different ways they are and have been loved, and all the different ways they are and have been failed.

Ben requested that no information about him be given to his family. We were devastated to have no word of him, but we were also grateful that his rights were recognized and respected.

In 2020, during the pandemic, the hospital called my parents to say that Ben would be transferred to a halfway house in Dublin. They desperately needed the bed, and they no longer deemed him a threat. Nevertheless, they advised my parents to alarm their home and take out a barring order against their son. After some time, my father spoke to the head of the house where Ben stays, and he was told that Ben was so intelligent and kind, so considerate and caring, and this is the Ben we all know and remember. We are grieving the loss of a brother, and a son, and an uncle, and a friend who might have been. Ben is still alive, but in a way that is unacceptable to us, so each of us must, in our own ways, confront our absolute powerlessness over this, and over so many situations in our lives.

Newgrange was built to mathematical and astronomical precision. Amazingly, it has remained waterproof in our rain-soaked land for the last five thousand years. In the early hours of the mornings around the winter solstice, if weather permits, a shaft of rising sunlight enters a small box above the doorway; it travels down the hallway and illuminates the inner chamber for approximately fourteen minutes.

Inside, there are three small chambers that held the remains of the dead. What were the ancestors thinking here? Were the dead to grow into new life, just as the day grows longer after the longest night? We cannot say for sure, but these architects clearly knew what we have forgotten: that we are deeply connected to those who came before, to those who are, and to those who will come after. We are connected by the dirt of the earth and the dust of the stars.

The mound is surrounded by large kerbstones, the most significant being the Entrance Stone with its tri-spiral designs. The engravings are similar to those of the native peoples of the American Great Plains and of other indigenous peoples: circles, spirals, arcs, triangles, zigzag patterns. What was the artist representing when she carved them? We can only imagine. Mountains? Waves? The ups and downs of life? The passing of time?

The last time I went there, our tour guide led us through the narrow hallway into the inner chamber. There were about eight of us standing comfortably inside, and after we examined the engravings and wondered at the mastery of the ceiling's corbelled vault structure, she said, "Now, I am going to turn out the lights." Suddenly, it was silent and cold, very dark and very full. Lungs breathing, hearts beating, blood flowing. *This is the womb of the world*, I thought. This place is as close as Ireland comes to a creation space, an *axis mundi*, a still point around which time turns.

This is not a recovery narrative. This is the story of a struggle with life on life's terms. Our ancestors had a different relationship to time. Time for them was cyclical rather than linear, so their stories do not follow a beginning, middle, and end structure. They allowed for many outcomes and many uncertainties. They knew they were powerless over the sun. They knew that even if it didn't rise as they hoped it would, life would still be teeming in the cold and dark inner chambers of the heart.

January
Notes on a Return

The past is the present, isn't it? It's the future too.
We all try to lie out of that but life won't let us.
—Eugene O'Neill, *Long Day's Journey into Night*

We did not plan to leave the US on the feast of Samhain, it just worked out that way. While the holiday is celebrated on the eve of October 31 through the eve of November 1, the actual astrological date for 2021, I read on my Mythical Ireland calendar, fell on November 7. How symbolic, I explained to Emmanuel, my partner of less than two years, that I should be returning to the native land on Celtic New Year. He is from Switzerland and, while he was glad to be leaving America for political reasons, he was less enchanted by the happy coincidence. For years, I wanted to move back to Ireland, but it always seemed an unattainable dream, to find the right time and the reserves of energy needed to gather up the life I had built, and move it back across the world. Then, suddenly, with a new relationship and a global pandemic, the move seemed not only entirely possible, but imminent and inevitable.

Emmanuel and I, disheartened by the overheated rental market in Ireland, even after living in New York City, began to look for an old house to buy. A home for ourselves and our two dogs. There were lots of abandoned cottages for sale with their St. Brigid's crosses and their faded pictures of the Sacred Heart still hanging askew on walls crumbling with mold. We would fix one up ourselves, we decided, because if viable candidates could not get a mortgage in the housing crisis, a couple of middle-aged, unemployed, returning emigrants were hardly likely to. The only place we could afford was a house in North Mayo, in the tiny township of Doonfeeny by the rugged Atlantic coast. We placed the successful bid on an online auction, never having seen the site. My family, my parents, my brothers and sisters, and my nieces and nephews drove the three hours from Ashbourne to spend their weekends fixing it up for our arrival. There was no electricity, or water or heat, they said. It had holes in the roof and moisture in the walls and floors. We had our work cut out. Please tell us something good, we pleaded, and they all said the same thing, that it was situated in, without a doubt, the most beautiful and strange and magical landscape they had ever seen.

For the Celtic people of Ireland, the year was divided into two halves. The light half and the dark half. The feast of Samhain initiates the dark half. This is the time of rest and death. This is the time when we remember those who have gone before, and in doing so, we are reminded that our present is in relationship with our past. Days before we left New York, with the remnants of Halloween and Día de los Muertos still evident in the supermarket candy aisles and the tattered skeletons decorating the neighborhood, Emmanuel sent me an article from the *New York Times*. It listed a couple of new additions to the International Dark Sky locations. These are places on the planet with little or no light pollution. Light pollution is described as excessive or misdirected outdoor light that wastes energy, disrupts ecosystems, and contributes to adverse health effects by causing dysregulation in circadian and diurnal rhythms. On further investigation, he had found that one of

Ireland's two designated locations is beside our new home. Thrilled by this news, I took it as further evidence that there was a secret synthesis guiding my return.

There are different kinds of return. There are journeys, internal and external, that some of us have to make to get to where we are going. I return again and again to the theme of the Famine. It is not conscious; I find myself hooked repeatedly into the stories of people's lives then, stories that fill the gaps in my imagination and in my family history. Take the life of James O'Neill, for example. He was born in County Kilkenny during the Great Hunger. His family emigrated to America, where his father took off and abandoned his wife and children. At the age of ten, young James had to leave school and go to work. He was acutely aware, in the way some poor kids are, of his lack of education, it ate away at him until he finally managed to get a tutor. He began reading Shakespeare and finding freedom in language. He worked hard to rid himself of his Irish accent so he could become a great actor, and he might have been, had the fear of the poorhouse not been etched into the forming fibers of his being. For financial security, he bought the rights to the popular play *The Count of Monte Cristo*, and performed it to sold-out theatres around the country. But as he played the same role night after night, year after year, he felt his talent grow dull and start to ebb, and he became a great drinker.

James and his wife, Mary Ellen Quinlan, had three children. The second child died of measles, and the young mother blamed her elder son for passing on the illness. Following the birth of her third child, still deep in grief, she became addicted to morphine.

This is the haunted house into which Eugene O'Neill was born in 1888. These family ghosts pursued him till the end of his life. Like his father and his brother, he was also an alcoholic, but he stopped drinking at the age of forty. Thirteen years later, after his family were long dead, he sat down to write his masterwork about them, *Long Day's Journey into Night*. To the character of Mary, who represented his mother, he gave the revelatory line, "The past is the present, isn't it? It's the future too." In some ways this story has its tragic roots in the Great Hunger and the pains we cannot outrun. It became O'Neill's best-known work, a day in the life of a family, a mirror of our own, with all their individual and interconnected sorrows and flaws and frailties laid bare.

Driving across Ireland from Dublin to Doonfeeny, Emmanuel is shocked by the presence of so many abandoned cottages, half-crumbling stone structures in fields along the roads. Why, he asks, do the farmers not knock them down? Surely they could use the land for grazing, and the stones for walls? Maybe the houses could be rebuilt and repurposed? Though we suspect they represent something deeper in the collective psyche. Perhaps they are symbols of unprocessed historical trauma, or symbols of the desire to live connected to, and alongside, the dead.

My family was right, the landscape of North Mayo is beautiful, strange, and magical. The neighboring village of Ballycastle centers around a main street with a couple of local shops, pubs, restaurants, a Catholic and a Protestant church, and a contemporary art museum. At the end of the street, hills rise up in bog-browns and greens, dotted intermittently with small white farmhouses and flecked here and there with clusters of sheep and cows. As we turn off to Doonfeeny and drive along the coast, the ocean comes into view and the atmosphere shifts again. It is wet and mutable; the sky expands and moves and changes from one second to the next, as if an invisible painter were in the process of composing it. Dragging a thick brush with grey paint quickly across a pale turquoise expanse. Then pressing down great daubs of purple, pink, and blue. Sprays of rain fall in distant patches, washing out and blurring sections, while in an instant the sun breaks through and a luminous rainbow might appear, disappear and reappear again. This sky is different every time you look at it, and you tear your eyes away only for the pleasure of returning to it.

There is a signpost pointing to Doonfeeny graveyard. It has a megalithic standing stone at its center. The five-thousand-year-old monument rises a triumphant fourteen feet out of the ground. There are Ogham inscriptions along its side. This early Irish alphabet was used between the fourth and the sixth centuries, and all its characters were the names of trees: oak, hazel, ash; you glimpse here something of the ancestral relationship to the natural world. Later, other craftspeople carved into the standing stone decorative Christian crosses of different eras. I run my fingers down one side, over the grey-green growth of lichen and moss. I

feel the years, the etching of history, the passing of time. The stone itself is believed to have been used in ancient fertility rites—no one can say for sure—but because it is pitched, according to the compass on my iPhone, due east, like all the graves in Ireland, to face the rising sun, it may have served another purpose. Perhaps it was an early calendar, or clock, a time-keeping device used by reading the shadows it cast on the earth around it.

Whatever the purpose of the standing stone, its placement here at the edge of the world, in clear and direct sight of the great cliff formations of Downpatrick

Head, certainly seems intentional. Especially in light of the fact that until the fourteenth century, when it crumbled in a great storm, there was a bridge that joined the sea stack of Dún Briste with the mainland. I look over and imagine that it might have looked like a portal to the ancestors who came here.

The names on the gravestones in the newer part of the cemetery are the same ones we see on the sides of work vans advertising trades, and above the local pub and shop doors. Heffernan, Burke, Langan. These families have been here for generations. Emmanuel and I are, and will always be, blow-ins, the strangers we had felt ourselves to be in our families and our hometowns, and later, in all the many places we passed through. But all that makes little difference to us now.

In the older part of the graveyard, the land buckles and sinks and old crosses are reclaimed by the earth. Most of the headstones are too worn to be read and others are marked by a simple rough stone. There are many famine stories from County Mayo, but one from this immediate area sticks with me. A local boy entered the cottage of an old widow who had a small bag of meal, and he murdered her violently for it. My heart grows heavy when I think of this boy and his family, and this widow and hers, and the tragedy of the whole starving lot of them.

I wonder what their ancestors, the ancient Brehons, would have made of the crime. They were Irish jurists and members of the priestly druid class who underwent a decades-long education period. They memorized, in the oral tradition, poetry, genealogy, history, magic, astronomy, and law. Brehon law was a restorative rather than a retributive system. Laws were not applied wholesale. Rather, each case was examined individually, and all factors relating to the parties involved were taken into consideration: their wealth, social standing, education, gender, ability, age, character, and so on. The Brehons' role was to guide the people and the overall goal of a judgement was to restore balance and harmony to the community. Brehon law was practiced throughout Ireland until the seventeenth century when Ireland was brought under British common law.

Now, when the old relationship to the natural world has been erased from view, perhaps the idea of balance and harmony can only exist as a distant memory. While it is easy to sanctify indigenous life and to overlook the challenges of living in the ancient world, it seems we might do well to remember that we carry these people inside us, and we might, in our moment, benefit from some acquaintance with their wisdom and ways.

> Landscape is not an objective area of land or coastline or bounded space; it is perceived individually through the lens of personal memory and depends on the accepted beliefs through which it is interpreted.

This is the opening of the text on the wall at Downpatrick Head, the impressive site that draws visitors from all over the world. These cliffs were formed 350 million years ago. It is a landscape carved out by the Cailleach, the creator goddess of deep time. She is the wise old woman of winter. She is immortal because she knows the secret of the darkest dark, which is that in it we find the eternal moment, the creative force that passes between life and death and death and life.

The Cailleach was there before the first memory and she will be there long after the last. She exists outside of time. She is neither fully good nor fully evil, in fact she will not conform to the simple dichotomies with which we tend to explain our world. She has no opinion about us devouring and destroying the earth.

She lives alone in a little hut and protects the creatures of the forest. On February 1 every year, she runs out of firewood. If the day is fine, she will go out and gather more, so winter can be prolonged. But if the day is dull, she will stay in bed, and as she relaxes back into sleep, she will loosen her grip, and she will let go a little, and little by little, winter will recede and the ground will soften, and Brigid will return.

It is true, I think, that the experience of landscape, and of everything in it and around it, is perceived individually through the lens of personal memory, and so it is strange being home. Uncanny sometimes. Other times, it is as if I never left. Nineties songs play on the ubiquitous Irish radio: in the garden center, at the café, at the post office and the bank. I sing along to UB40, Enya, REM.

Sunday Mass in Ballycastle was like stepping into a time-warp. I find myself at the end of the journey of writing this book, where I began, in a church named for St. Brigid. I am surrounded by the faces and features that penetrated my consciousness when I was a child: a tight-lipped woman in her good coat; a

broad-necked man with his three young children, their
clean clothes and their freshly washed hair gleaming.
There was a woman about my age who looked like a
girl I went to school with—though my hometown is
on the other side of the country. That girl married her
first boyfriend and they bought a house close to her
parents, had a few children and worked locally around
Ashbourne. The woman in the church stood in a
middle pew beside her aged mother. Their bodies were
the same shape. Their jawlines. Their soft, sad eyes.
The old, visiting priest mumbled along, and I didn't
understand a word, but I let the muscle memory take
over and guide my responses, when to sit and kneel
and stand, when to bow my head and when to lift it
up again. It is something to return now, and to feel
what it is to walk out with a congregation on a Sunday
morning onto a grey street under a grey sky spitting
rain and to wonder, for a moment, if the last thirty
years of my life even happened at all.

My family had cleaned the house up and filled it with
everything they thought we might need: Blankets, an
electric kettle, cups for tea, a pot, and tins of soup.

Their care, and our grateful acceptance of it, signaled the beginning of a deeper, more involved relationship between all of us. On the night we arrived, we walked outside with the dogs, Francis and Basil, and we saw that it was indeed very dark. We could hear nothing but the breathing of the great Atlantic Ocean, whose tides rolled between the shores of our old lives and our new one. It makes sense that the word "tide"—from the Old English *tīd*, means a measure of time. Henri Bergson was right, any measure of time, no matter how you slice it, nanoseconds, days, light years, is always interconnected and always flowing.

We could see the stars—I mean really see them—a trillion points of light piercing the dark velvet dome. It costs nothing to stand where we are and look up, and to think about how we are connected to all that has gone before, and to remember that our future, while not yet written, will arise out of this moment. It is something to go on journey, whether it is down the road or halfway around the world, and it is something else to return, and to stand, feet planted, and know that, at least in this moment, you are exactly where you are meant to be.

Works Cited and Consulted

"Alarm Will Sound", Iarla Ó Lionáird and Katherine Manley. *The Hunger*. Composed by Donnacha Dennehy. Directed by Tom Creed. Sept. 30, 2016. Brooklyn Academy of Music, New York, NY.

Berger, John. "Twelve Theses on the Economy of the Dead." *Left Curve*. Issue 31. Sept. 2007.

Berger, Shelley. Perelman School of Medicine at the University of Pennsylvania. https://www.pennmedicine.org

Bergson, Henri-Louis. *Time and Free Will: An Essay on the Immediate Data of Consciousness*. Dover, 2001.

of Bingen, St. Hildegard. "Part 1. Vision 1." *The Book of Divine Works*. Tr. Nathaniel M. Campbell. The Catholic University of America Press, 2018.

Boland, Eavan. "Mother Ireland." *The Lost Land*. Norton, 1998. Reprinted by permission.

Brontë, Charlotte. *Charlotte Brontë: An Independent Will*. The Morgan Library & Museum. New York, NY, Sept. 30, 2016–Jan 2, 2017.

Burroughs, William S. *The Naked Lunch*. Grove, 1959.

Can't Cope, Won't Cope. Directed by Cathy Brady and Imogen Murphy. Deadpan Pictures. Netflix, 2018.

Eugene O'Neill: A Documentary Film. Directed by Ric Burns. Steeplechase Films. American Experience, PBS, 2006.

Carson, Anne. *Nox*. New Directions, 2010.

Cline, Patsy. "Crazy." *Showcase*. Written by Willie Nelson. Decca Records, 1961. Vinyl.

Cooper Owens, Deirdre. *Medical Bondage: Race, Gender and the Origins of American Gynecology*. University of Georgia Press, 2017.

Costandi, Mo. "Pregnant 9/11 Survivors Transmitted Trauma to their Children", *Guardian*, 9 Sept. 2011. https://www.theguardian.com/science/neurophilosophy/2011/sep/09/pregnant-911-survivors-transmitted-trauma

Davis, Miles. *Kind of Blue*. Concord Music Group, 1959. CD.

Didion, Joan. *The White Album*. Simon & Schuster, 1979.

Didion, Joan. *The Year of Magical Thinking*. Reprinted by Permission of HarperCollins Ltd © 2006, Joan Didion.

Dwyer, Jim. "At St. Brigid's A Life Lost, Though Not Unknown." *New York Times*, Feb. 22, 2011. https://www.nytimes.com/2011/02/23/nyregion/23about.html

Eagleton, Terry. "Angry 'Un." *London Review of Books*. No. 13, Vol. 15, Jul. 8, 1993.

Emmet, Thomas Addis. *Reminiscences of the Founders of the Woman's Hospital Association.* Stuyvesant Press, 1893.

French, Brett. "Expeditions of Excess." *Billings Gazette.* Oct. 9, 2002 https://billingsgazette.com/news/features/outdoors/expedition-of-excess/article_fe245dc0-67e6-5689-ae80-d451696472ce.html

Freud, Sigmund. "Mourning and Melancholia." *Collected Papers, Vol. IV.* Tr. Joan Riviere. Hogarth Press and The Institute of Psychoanalysis, 1950. pp. 152–70.

"Grace & Emmanuel." *Documentary on One.* Produced by Michael Kealy and Ronan Kelly. RTÉ Radio 1. July 18, 2015 (21:00–22:00).

Hirsch, Marianne. "Marked by Memory." *Extremities: Trauma, Testimony, Community* Eds. Nancy K. Miller and Jason Tougaw. Illinois University Press, 2002.

Hirsch, Marianne. *Generation of Postmemory.* Columbia University Press, 2012.

Hogan, G.W. "Law and Religion: Church–State Relations in Ireland from Independence to the Present Day." *The American Journal of Comparative Law.* Vol. 35, No. 1. Oxford University Press, 1987. pp. 47–96.

Irigaray, Luce. "When our Lips Speak Together." *Signs.* Vol. 6, No. 1. Women: Sex and Sexuality, Part 2. Tr. Carolyn Burke. University of Chicago Press, 1980. pp. 69–79.

Irish Hunger Memorial. https://www.nyc.com/arts__attractions/irish_hunger_memorial.1379/

Irish Mission at Watson House. "The Untold Story of the Home for Irish Immigrant Girls in Lower Manhattan, 1883–1954." Archives of the Archdiocese of New York. Digital Collections. Available: http://omeka.archnyarchives.org/exhibits/show/missiongirls/intro.

Jung, Carl G. *The Red Book*. Ed. Sonu Shamdasani. Philemon, 2009.

Jung, Carl G. *Memories, Dreams, Reflections*. Ed. Aniela Jaffé. Vintage, 1989.

Kinealy, Christine. *The Great Calamity: The Irish Famine 1845–52*. Gill & Macmillan, 1994.

Magan, Manchán and Antic Ham. *Sea Tamagotchi*. Red Fox, 2020.

Maté, Dr. Gabor. CRAZYWISE Interview. May 24, 2014. https://www.youtube.com/watch?v=-xzP_9-Y2qg.

McAleese, Martin. *Report of the Inter-Departmental Committee to Establish the Facts of State Involvement with the Magdalen Laundries*. 2013. http://www.justice.ie/en/JELR/Pages/MagdalenRpt2013

Miller, Henry. *Tropic of Capricorn*. Flamingo, 1993.

Monaghan, Patricia. *The Encyclopedia of Celtic Mythology and Folklore*. Checkmark, 2010.

Works Cited and Consulted

Monaghan, Patricia. *Brigit: Sun of Womanhood*. Goddess Ink, 2013.

Notley, Alice. "To My Father." *Phoebe Light*. Big Sky Books, 1973. Reprinted by permission.

O'Callaghan, Jeremiah. "Skibereen." Famine Report. *Cork Examiner*. 18 Dec. 1846.

O'Neill, Eugene. *Long Day's Journey into Night*. Nick Hern Books, 1991. Reprinted by permission.

Pollak, Sorcha, "Woman Buried Without Friends Present after Death in Direct Provision Centre." *Irish Times*, June 7. 2019. https://www.irishtimes.com/news/social-affairs/woman-buried-without-friends-present-after-death-in-direct-provision-centre-1.3917038.

Sims, J. Marion. *The Story of My Life*. D. Appleton and Company, 1886.

Smith, Ailbhe. *The Abortion Papers Ireland: Vol. 2*. Eds. Conlon, Kennedy, Quilty. Attic Press, 2016.

Spence, Clark C. "A Celtic Nimrod in the Old West." *The Montana Magazine of Western History*. Vol. 9, No.2. Montana Historical Society, 1959. pp. 56–66.

Thomas Addis Emmet Papers. Misc. Correspondence with Worthington C. Ford and Sabin 1890–95. The Brooke Russell Astor Reading Room for Rare Books and Manuscripts. Manuscripts, Archives and Rare Books. The New York Public Library. Oct. 17, 2019.

Thompson, Flora. "'Failed by the State' – President Michael D. Higgins apologizes to women forced to work in Magdalene laundries." *Irish Independent*. June 5, 2018. https://www.independent.ie/irish-news/news/failed-by-the-state-president-michael-d-higgins-apologises-to-women-forced-to-work-in-magdalene-laundries-36981158.html.

Tippett, Krista. "How Trauma and Resilience Cross Generations." Interviewee Dr. Rachel Yehuda, PhD. *On Being from NPR,* July 30, 2015. https://onbeing.org/programs/rachel-yehuda-how-trauma-and-resilience-cross-generations-nov2017/

Van der Kolk, Bessel. *The Body Keeps the Score*. Penguin, 2014.

Violent Femmes. "Blister in the Sun." Slash, 1983.

Waheed, Nayyirah. "Lands." *Salt*. CreateSpace Independent Publishing Platform, 2013.

Washington, Harriet A. *Medical Apartheid: The Dark History of Medical Experimentation on Black Americans from Colonial Times to the Present*. Anchor, 2008.

Woman's Hospital Association Meetings 1855–1863. Arthur H. Aufses, Jr., MD Archives. Icahn School of Medicine, New York, NY. Oct. 31, 2019.

Woman's Hospital Patient Casebooks: J. Marion Sims 1855–1861 and Sims/Emmet 1859–1868. Arthur H. Aufses, Jr., MD Archives. Icahn School of Medicine, New York, NY. Oct. 31, 2019.

Woman's Hospital Records 1855–1952. Arthur H. Aufses, Jr., MD Archives. Icahn School of Medicine, New York, NY. Oct. 31, 2019.

Woolf, Virginia. *On Being Ill*. Wesleyan University Press, 2012.

Woolf, Virginia. *Mrs. Dalloway*. Harcourt, 1981.

Woolf, Virginia. *A Passionate Apprentice: The Early Journals 1897–1909*. Ed. Mitchell Alexander Leaska. Harcourt Brace Jovanovich, 1990.

Rachel Yehuda and Amy Lerner. "Intergenerational Transmission of Trauma effects: Putative Role of Epigenetic Mechanisms." *World Psychiatry*. Vol. 17, Issue. 3. Wiley Online Library. p. 24.